FURTHER
GUIDELINES FOR ART EDUCATION

Key Stages 1–5

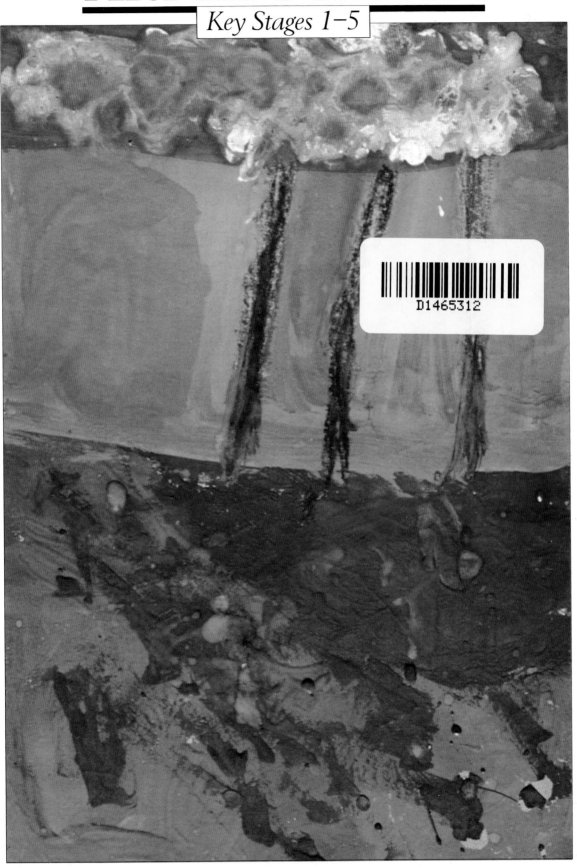

Above: *Key Stage 5 – The use of visual dynamics has helped the pupil explore the concepts of energy and movement.*

Previous Page: *Key Stage 1 – A pupil makes an immediate response to a walk in the woods.*

Foreword

This publication builds on the excellent foundations of the 1986 guidelines and accommodates the requirements of the National Curriculum. It has been planned to link with the publication of National Curriculum for art but we should recall the role art can play throughout the curriculum. Art comprises clearly identified sets of knowledge, understanding, skills and techniques in almost any medium but it can contribute to and be drawn from many other parts of the curriculum. There are clear opportunities for art to support learning throughout the curriculum. The skills and understanding developed through art will also extend the young students' thinking and feelings.

Art is essentially creative; developing, revealing, interpreting and simulating emotions as well as thoughts in the viewer and creator. It reminds us continually of the range and depth of the education process and its effects on the whole person. That is the essence of the responsibility of teachers and of all involved in education.

Such people put together these excellent guidelines. This very committed group of teachers cover all parts of primary, secondary and tertiary education. They were inspired by Lorna Delaney's work on the 1986 guidelines. Maurice Barrett again presented papers with commitment and passion. Mary Schley, County Art Inspector and Wendy Richardson, Teacher Adviser for Art have steered and been integral to this creative process, and the County and the team owe a great deal to Mary's management of the publication.

Hampshire County Council support the Arts in many ways. Those working in the field take encouragment from this and I have no doubt that the value we place on creative activities help young people know themselves, realise their potential and understand the world better. That is the purpose of all our efforts.

PETER COLES
County Education Officer

Acknowledgements

These guidelines reflect the commitment to education through art from people directly involved with education, to those who may be associated with it as administrators, organisers or receivers. So many people have contributed to the work that words cannot adequately express gratitude.

We are indebted to Lorna Delaney who, through her vision and inspiration, saw the need for further development. Despite the nearness of her retirement she began the process for the Further Guidelines for Art Education. Lorna's ability to encourage and monitor, to value the strength and uniqueness of each individual has been a source of inspiration, determination and unity to all involved in art education.

The continual support of Hampshire's Education Department is testimony to their belief in the value of the arts in education. Without their financial support, encouragement and guidance no aspect of the Guidelines could have taken place.

Maurice Barrett, the author of the discussion papers, has continued to inspire us with his vision and passion for education and art. In presenting the papers he invited questioning, probing and testing. He never tires of listening and reflecting and will readily admit that Hampshire teachers have been a formative learning experience. As joint editors, Wendy Richardson and I would like to thank Maurice for permitting the editing of his papers for our use in Hampshire.

I am sure that Hampshire teachers would wish to join me in expressing our gratitude to Wendy Richardson, the Teacher Adviser for art. Through the in-service training of teachers, now reaching many thousands in number, she has promoted our concept of art in education and has begun with the dissemination of these guidelines. We thank her for the many hours she has devoted to this and to guidelines.

Our thanks to Ray Hyden, director of 'Type Generation'. His calm patience, guidance, gentle but poignant prompting for deadlines and sheer hard work were worth it.

The illustrations in these guidelines are from schools throughout the county. They are proof of the healthy existence of art education. We thank those schools' pupils and artists; (Andy Prost, Robert Jakes, Anthony Lysycia, Polly Pollock and Southern Arts touring exhibition service Finch group) who have allowed us to use their work.

I wish to thank my secretary Linda Cutter who forged her way through teachers' scribbled drafts to the final manuscript with unstinting patience and perseverance.

Our thanks to husbands, wives, partners and families who tolerated the intrusion of many weekends, Saturdays and evenings. Without their support our goals could not have been realised.

Those most closely involved are listed alphabetically; they represent all key stages in education and they include Headteachers, Heads of Departments and Assistant teachers.

Andrea Badkin, Sonia Barrett, Joan Benning, Daphne Caless, Marilyn Campbell, Derek Cheshire, Maureen Cooding, Stephanie Crisp, Francis Dimmer, Tony Dimmer, Maggie Elson, Hilary Flaxman, Linda Fredericks, Sheila Goucher, Cathy Hales, Linda Hay, Ken Kenyon, Olwyn Phillips, Tina Maxwell, Audree Mendham, Adrian Postle, David Thomas,

Thank you to all involved. M.S.

Contents

Introduction

As we witness a period of change and reform in education it is fitting and timely that the publication of Hampshire's Further Guidelines for Art Education will coincide with the publication of the National Curriculum for art.

This book builds on the foundation laid in the first "Guidelines for Art Education" published in 1986 under the leadership of former County Art Adviser, Lorna Delaney. The foundation dealt with the nature of art and with the practical learning processes of art and design.

In these Guidelines the discussion papers and teachers' discussions consider the issues behind an art curriculum. The issues address four key areas which are relevant to the quality of teaching and learning in art and which are pertinent to the planning and delivery of the National Curriculum for art.

As with the first Guidelines, Maurice Barrett, retired Art Adviser for Redbridge and now freelance consultant, wrote and presented the four papers which have formed the theoretical framework of the book. Teachers, grouped in key stages, have sought to clarify the nature of appropriate experiences for children in their key stage; thus identifying progression and continuity from five to eighteen.

The four sections in these guidelines may be considered in isolation but they are, in practice, inextricably linked.

- The relationship of evaluation and assessment to the realisation of art as a tool for learning and as a means by which we know reality.

- Appropriate experiences for the development of aesthetic sensitivity and critical awareness.

- The use of visual language (line, tone, colour, shape, texture and form), as a developing means of communication.

- The relationship between artistic and functional design – a need highlighted by the emphasis in the National Curriculum on design and technology.

These Guidelines are less concerned with the assessment of children as a formal activity and concentrate more on the value of the process of learning through and in art. Whilst we recognise that there is much in art which is open to objective assessment, we have also dealt with those elements of the subject which are concerned with the development of imagination, creativity, personal values, attitudes and judgements.

The proposals for the National Curriculum have placed art firmly as a foundation subject. The ensuing debate as to the nature and content of an art curriculum have provoked issues which need careful consideration and in which teachers of all phases of education are seeking guidance. It is hoped that the thinking behind the papers presented here, and the teachers' discussions, will help other teachers clarify their own ideas and beliefs, give their practice personal direction and meaning, and help them cope effectively with the requirements of the National Curriculum for art.

As with the first guidelines, a group of teachers, not chosen as art experts but representing teaching expertise from all key stages of education, have formed the working party. Hampshire Education Department's in-service training provision, in the form of residential courses, once again provided the opportunity for the writing of these guidelines. The material for the book has been tried, tested and modified by members of the working group over a period of three years. We know that those of us who have been involved in this production are privileged. As a team we have shared and tested our expertise as teachers. Words cannot describe the laughter and humour, the doubts and anxieties, and the fierce discussions we have held about philosophy of art, philosophy of education, and the implications for art and for society in a changing educational system. We have been involved in experiential learning, gaining from each others expertise and the value and respect we have for each other.

We have, after pondering long and hard, decided to use the word "pupil" throughout all key stages. This simplifies any possible confusion between key stages four and five. Within the teachers' discussions a key stage is often referred to as a "phase". This felt less clumsy and more sympathetic towards the recognition of children's developmental stages.

In a climate of change, increasing demands are being made on teachers' professional understanding and competence. These guidelines stem from Lorna Delaney's conviction, shared with the working party, and many other teachers that art education should provide children with experiential learning about themselves in their world. Art provides a unique means of learning, understanding and communicating, and in this way is significant to the whole curriculum and to the child.

We hope that these guidelines will provide a resource for teachers' own development, and through art, enrich children's understanding of themselves in their world.

Mary Schley
County Inspector for art

SECTION I

Evaluation and Assessment
by Maurice Barrett

The evaluation of all aspects of learning is central to good teaching. The worthwhile outcomes of education can only be maintained and fostered if evaluation of processes and products is undertaken by children and teachers. All successful teaching depends upon the evaluation of evidence. Many teachers are highly skilled in its subtleties. It is an integral part of the learning process. Teachers are continuously involved with evaluation and assessment, engaging in discussions, questioning, supporting and helping children make their own decisions.

Evaluation is an integral part of the process of art. Continuous critical appraisal of the creative process is essential to any artistic activity. Without qualitative evaluation of the processes there can be no hope for a successful outcome measured against the criteria developed and embodied within the work.

Teachers are continuously involved with evaluating the process and product of the teaching and learning activities. But it is essential that evaluation serves education and is not only seen as a means of satisfying needs which are extrinsic to the learning process.

As the methods of art education are various and flexible, there would be very little point in prescribing a single strategy for assessment and evaluation. Teachers will need to consider the most effective ways to ensure that the methods used for assessment and evaluation are directly related to their teaching and learning strategies. These will vary between schools, phases and subject areas, and will reflect the particular educational concept which determines the procedures and the criteria.

The purpose of this section of guidelines is to reinforce good practice and to map out the broad terrain of evaluation and assessment. Teachers will be able to identify their own procedures and extend their practice by recognising alternative approaches.

This section will try to work across a broad context attempting to clarify the purpose of evaluation and assessment for the pupil as well as for the teacher. Discussions have related to the principles set down by the Hampshire Assessment and Recording of Achievement Team (HARAT). The special nature of art, craft and design requires a particular focus.

Issues to be Considered
An appropriate model
In Hampshire's Guidelines for Art Education 5-18[1] the process model (see p.13) was adopted as the most appropriate framework. To create a framework it is necessary to identify activities which seem to have inherent worth and are accessible to the judgement and understanding of others. These need to be set out in a form which is acceptable to art teachers and their colleagues in other disciplines. This process model appears to satisfy both requirements.

Art, like other forms of knowledge, has its own structure of concepts, procedures and criteria. It is through an understanding of these that art can be comprehended as a whole. There can be no finite understanding of art, for at any level, the concepts, procedures, and criteria are the focus of speculation, not the object of ultimate mastery. This is part of the essential nature of the subject. Art is not just a body of knowledge, a skill, a set of rules, or a process. The sum of all our visual knowledge is not only what we know, but the way we know it and respond to it. Commitment to this idea is the crucial concern of art education.

Definitions
For the purpose of these guidelines it should be understood that these definitions are not fixed but are only used for the purpose of simplification and clarification.

Assessment is used to mean the judgement of a process or a product against a range of clearly defined criteria. It is used in the same way as the National Criteria for Art and Design[2] when defining "assessable objectives". The pre-requisite for assessment when adopting this

Key Stage 1

Key Stage 2

Key Stage 3

Key Stages 4/5

"The sum of our visual knowledge is not only what we know but the way we know it and respond to it."

definition is that the concept, procedure and criteria are understood and shared by pupils and teachers. This definition assumes a high degree of objectivity within the criteria.

Evaluation is used to mean the judgement of process or product, within a framework of values, which are personal or shared through the negotiation of some particular meaning. In this definition subjectivity is as important as objectivity. The values are more open to negotiation and are flexible. They are more applicable to judgement by criteria which are embodied within the work.

Formative evaluation or assessment is concerned with the continuing process. It is diagnostic, exploratory, it is "a vital lubricant in the dynamics of learning" Devon Working Party on Assessment of Achievement[3]. It is the means by which the pupil or teacher monitor the process or product as they develop. It is the evaluation of the past and present and a guide for the future.

Summative evaluation or assessment is a summation of achievement at the end of a process and/or the completion of achievement.

Both formative and summative evaluations of art are an essential aspect of the artistic process, not a "bolt-on" separate activity.

Formative assessment and evaluation are concerned with process, formation and development. The emphasis is upon the on-going process of learning and the pupils' progress within this. Its main purpose is to diagnose future learning needs and strategies.

Summative assessment and evaluation is concerned with providing overall evidence of ability and achievement. It is the summation of achievement at the end of a process of learning. Veronica Treacher in "Assessment and Evaluation in the Arts"[4] draws attention to a strong divergence of views:

"... between those who consider educational process and formative diagnostic assessment as important for improving quality and those who thought that imposing external standards was the first pre-requisite."

This dichotomy is at the heart of the problems related to evaluation and assessment. It is concerned with the question of whether these aspects of education are intrinsic or extrinsic to the process. Is evaluation an integrated part of the process of extending and developing the learning? or is it a means of measuring the levels of success or failure related to the teacher's (or society's) views of anticipated outcomes? Both approaches play an important part in any educational strategy. It is important to understand the differences between the functions in order to avoid any confusion which may invalidate their particular use.

Evaluation and Child Development

Children in different phases of learning will respond differently in the ways that they evaluate and appraise their work. Whilst it is generally accepted that there are different ways of knowing at different stages of development, it must also be realised that there are different qualities of appraisal associated with these stages.

Eileen Pickard in her study 'The Development of Creative Ability'[5] says:

"The child who falls generally into the concrete operational period of development has attained a significant degree of cognitive organisation, but he is still bounded by the immediate, ill at ease in the world of the hypothetical and better able to deal with things than ideas. As these conditions affect his constructions of reality so too they circumscribe his reconstructions. To construct and reconstruct reality with understanding of the processes involved, an individual must be capable of reflecting upon knowledge and the process of knowing. In other words he must be Piaget's formal operational thinker. Capable of understanding reality as organised and interpreted by a given culture and of self as an interpreter of reality, this thinker has the consciousness which is critical to mature constructions and reconstructions of reality."

Children working through concrete operations, not able to hypothesise will appraise their own work, and the work of others, in terms of immediate perceptions, using comparison, contrasting, selecting, focussing and valuing in terms of a direct response. As children mature and develop into formal abstract operations their ability to hypothesise will allow them to make suppositions and assumptions through the interrelationship of different aspects of their knowledge and experience.

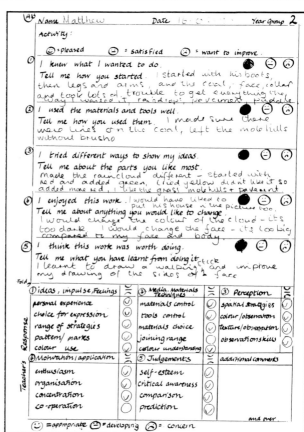

Key Stage 1 – "I would change the colour of the cloud – it's too dark. I would change the face – it's too big compared to my face and body."

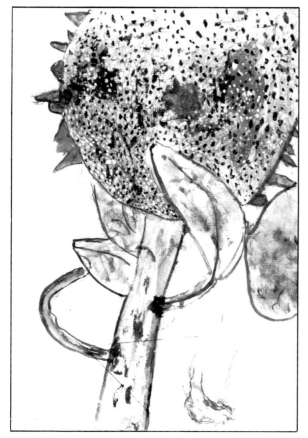

Key Stage 2 – "I drew the pattern of the sunflower seeds well but the paint spoilt it."

Key Stage 3 – "The plaster set very quickly. Although the the legs are wobbly the figures look as though they are playing leapfrog."

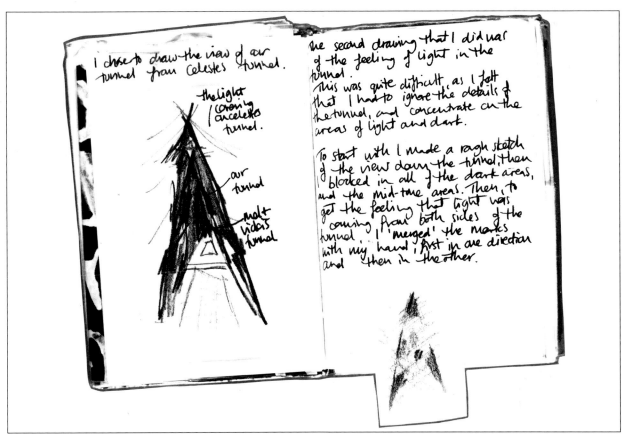

Key Stage 5 – Annotated notes in a sketchbook.

In the same book Eileen Pickard says:

"Evaluation implies consciousness of one's own activity and of the outcome of the activity and an ability to make judgements about both in the light of one's understanding of knowledge."

Younger children will evaluate on the basis of direct concrete responses to experiences. They should not be expected to respond to the subtle cultural nuances of adult art. They are unlikely to make culturally determined aesthetic judgements which coincide with the views of their elders. They are more likely to respond to identifiable content, for example "I like that tree" and "that's a pretty colour". They may view a fine art painting in the same way as a photograph and a Rembrandt portrait in the same way as a pop pin-up. This is not to diminish their evaluative appraisal; it is to refer to the differences in the nature of the operation. See Section III; Aesthetic Sensitivity and Critical Studies.

Sharing Criteria

The pupils' evaluation of their work is crucially important in art. The teachers' evaluation of the pupils' work must include a consideration of the pupils' ability to evaluate the process and product of their own work. In order to be able to assist in the progressive development of the work, the teacher and pupil will have to negotiate and understand the criteria they are using. Part of the learning process is to build personal criteria progressively within a framework of shared criteria. These will become increasingly complex as knowledge, understanding and experience accumulate. They will become the means through which the learning strategies are negotiated. This mutually evaluative process is central to teaching and learning. In art the pupils' perception of the learning process is the starting point for teaching.

Objective and Subjective Assessment

In the process of evaluating art there is the problem of whether it is essentially a subjective process or whether it is open to objective appraisal. Without doubt there must be elements of subjectivity in the process of creating and evaluating art. This occurs when the response to any sensory experience is individual and personal in so far as there is no wish to appraise against external criteria. Subjective evaluation is valid for the individual who makes it, and may be shared with, and appreciated by others. Objective evaluation requires the recognition of external criteria which are relevant to

Key Stage 1 – The pupil responded directly to the task by recording the pattern and shape in the building.

the artifact being appraised, and to its social and cultural context.

It is important for the teacher to ascertain whether the pupils are best approached through their subjective responses, or assisted through those values which are shared, or held in common, which will be more objective. There are obviously objective aspects of the arts which are open to assessment but teachers should keep in mind the very clear statements in the National Criteria for Art and Design(2).

"The aims given below set out the following educational purposes for following a course in art and design...... They include references to a number of attributes and qualities which cannot or should not be assessed for examination purposes but which nevertheless form an essential part of any Art and Design course. In this respect the aims differ from the assessment objectives which all refer to qualities and competencies to be assessed."

A clear distinction is made between qualities which are an essential aspect of art education

Key Stage 1 – The subjective response which shows that the pupil's interest in the plants has overriden the task of looking at patterns and shapes in the building.

Key Stage 3 – Objective criteria – a line drawing of figures which fill the page.

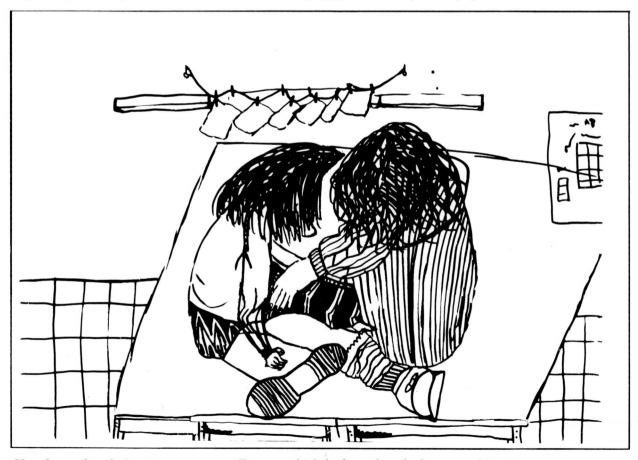

Key Stage 3 – Subjective response – Figures which look as though they are whispering.

Key Stage 1 – Constraints which relate to the learning objectives; constraint of materials to help pupils focus on pattern.

Key Stage 3 – Constraint of time, working quickly to focus on rhythm and movement of figure.

but not open to objective assessment and those shared values which are open to objective assessment. Although these statements are made in reference to a secondary school examination, it is a valuable starting point for any consideration of evaluation and assessment in the arts.

This issue will continue to divide arts educators. It is inescapable that there are many aspects of art concerned with objective knowledge of the historical, biographical, sociological, anthropological, and cultural kind which can be objectively assessed. But competence in these areas is essentially different from aesthetic and artistic learning. This is concerned with giving visual form to our ideas, feelings and perceptions through the manipulation of media, materials and techniques. This does not invalidate the former but it does require a different perspective of the process of evaluation. An emphasis on objective and cognitive aspects of art as a social and cultural activity may provide valuable indicators of a pupil's ability to appraise within a particular frame of reference, but this is different in form and nature from the evaluation of the practical process and product of art.

Freedom or Control

One of the most difficult problems that teachers have to resolve is concerned with the balance between the pupils' freedom to explore and respond to experiences and the need to develop the appropriate learning skills. To do this the teacher should be able to make explicit those criteria which will be used as a basis for teaching through the arts.

These should be made clear and used appropriately to sustain and support the pupils' work but they should not become a control imposed upon the pupils' imaginative and creative activities. There needs to be a careful balance between freedom and control. This can be achieved by the continuous involvement of the pupil and the teacher in formative evaluation. Too much freedom and reliance upon personal qualitative values will leave the pupil confused and culturally disorientated. Too much control will result in the death of art and creativity.

Absolute criteria will be the death of art in the same way as absolute freedom would be destructive and pointless. Continuous monitoring, evaluation and negotiated learning are the best ways to maintain a balance between the two extremes.

A Framework for Evaluation and Assessment

The process model can be used as a basis for evaluation and assessment. It enables the pupil to monitor the formative process and the teacher to ensure the maintenance of a balanced curriculum in art and design. The "concept" element of the process model for art is comprised of three interrelated and reflexive elements.

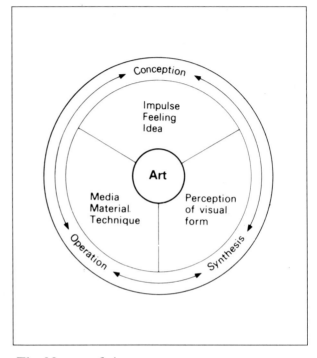

The Nature of Art.

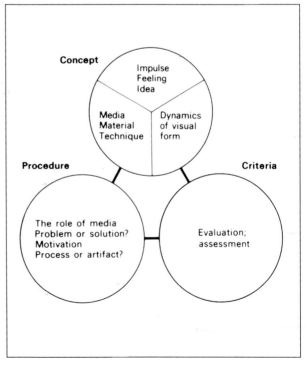

The Process Model.

The conceptual element concerned with ideas, perceptions, feelings, impulses and responses.

The operational element concerned with the control and use of techniques, materials and media.

The synthetic element concerned with the perception of the dynamics of visual language, line, tone, colour, texture, movement, structure and form.

To be dynamically effective in creativity and art another element is essential. It is an integrating tension between the elements and between these and the artist, and between the artist and the context of community and culture.

In evaluating the pupil's ability, aptitude and achievement in the process and product of his or her work, other aspects may need to be considered. An extended range was set out in "Art in Secondary Education, 11-16" (DES)[6]:

Involvement	1. Interest and Enjoyment
	2. Practical skills
Concept	3. The ability to express ideas visually
	4. The ability to make aesthetic judgements
	5. The ability to observe, record and interpret
Graphicacy & making	6. The ability to transpose from 2 to 3 dimensional and vice versa
Involvement	7. The ability to work co-operatively

Items 2, 3 and 4 relate roughly to the concept element within the process model. (See page 13 The Nature of Art). Item 3 relates to "Ideas, impulses, feelings and perceptions". Item 2 relates to "materials, media and techniques". Item 4 relates to "the dynamics of visual form". Items 1 and 7 are concerned with the quality of involvement and 5 and 6 emphasise the overriding importance of graphicacy and making. In evaluating the process and product of art it is essential to consider the pupil's values, attitudes, judgements and responses as well as the expressive and academic aspects.

Evaluation fulfils many functions. It can be seen in the contexts of examination, achievement of attainment targets, pupil profiles, records of achievement, critical appraisal and other formal and informal aspects of education. It can help to diagnose problems and suggest areas of future development. It can be concerned with objective standards as well as personal values. When the evaluation of the pupil is allied to the evaluation of process and product, issues of motivation, application and concentration enter the range of criteria. Thus art and education are jointly assessed.

There is also the need to determine the degree to which the pupil is capable of self-evaluation, self-appraisal and self-motivation. Evaluation should be concerned with personal as well as academic development. It should not only be a means of assessment of the pupil, but for the pupil. The curriculum can be modified in the light of continuous monitoring and evaluation. We must ask not only what we need to know as teachers but what the pupils need to know about themselves. They want to know what is expected of them and to what extent they have achieved it. They need their level of understanding to be known and catered for. They need to know what they are expected to do and how effectively they can do it. But above all, they need to understand and share the criteria by which they can be evaluated. This applies to all key stages of education.

The Means and Methods – When and How do we Evaluate?

The evaluation of the processes and products of art education takes place at different times for a variety of reasons. To clarify some of these may help the teacher to realise how the evaluative process is integrated within the teaching strategies.

The seven sections set out below attempt to define the range of evaluation and assessment. The essential element which pervades all of them is that evaluation and assessment are integral to the process of learning through art and design. They are also an integral part of the learning process and as such require both the pupil and the teacher to be involved. As the processes and criteria become progressively complex the teacher must enable the evaluative process and criteria to be kept in tune with the working process and its outcomes. All education is best when it is progressively collaborative.

Formative Evaluation – Pupil/Teacher – Direction Interaction

This is the most common form experienced by both pupil and teacher. In a one-to-one situation the art process can be discussed and evaluated. The most effective entry is through the pupils' evaluative response to the work at their own level. It may be purely subjective or call upon shared knowledge and experience. The teacher can foster the evaluative processes through questions related to the way the child works and what has been made. Successive questions should take account of previous statements and should encourage the pupil to question and explore. As the exchange of questions and answers clarifies the pupil's involvement, the teacher will be able to decide whether to give positive objective guidance or to develop the pupil's perception through the extension of experience. A direct objective question by the pupil answered directly by the teacher may assume pupil self-evaluation. However this could become a form of didactic teaching lacking the benefit of evaluative learning.

Art and education can only take place when both pupil and teacher are continuously involved within the evaluation of process and product. This can then form a basis for negotiated learning allowing for both freedom and control.

Formative Evaluation – Group/Teacher – Direct Interaction

This form of evaluation is more concerned with the teacher's strategy for learning. On the basis of continual contact with individual pupils or through group discussion, the teacher is able to evaluate how effectively the group is responding to the work in hand. Do they understand? Is it within their range of ability? Is their interest being sustained? When is the time to extend the task? Is there a need for clarification? Do they need objective guidance?

On many occasions the teacher is able to judge from the evidence of the group's process and product. On other occasions there may be a need to recapitulate and involve the group in the formative evaluation. This type of group evaluation can help the pupil to understand the nature and range of the criteria related to the process in hand. This will foster the development of personal appraisal and the evaluation of their own work in process. This is necessary in an arts activity where the individual's options are open. The level of freedom or control must be carefully monitored to avoid anarchy on one hand or group conformity on the other.

Formative Evaluation – Pupil/Teacher – Longer term

Apart from the continuous and immediate evaluation of process and work, there needs to be periodic recapitulation of activities within an evaluative framework. This could take place at the end of a particular piece of work, within a project, or at the end of a project before embarking on some form of extension. It is essential for children to develop an understanding of the value of immediate and longer term evaluation, so that they are able to see their work and plan further activities within a widening perspective. They will be more able to do this if their personal evaluation is made within a framework developed through the knowledge and experience the teacher has of the pupils.

Formative Evaluation – Group/Teacher – Longer Term

The curriculum should be negotiated between the professional knowledge and expertise of the teacher and the needs, aptitudes and abilities of the pupils. Ideally a separate learning strategy would be devised for each pupil. But the pressure created by school organisation and curriculum often requires the teacher to see each individual within the context of a group, community, culture and gender. By evaluating past work the pupils and teachers are more able to negotiate the most effective way forward. Again we have the problem of freedom and control. This is best resolved through the group's ability to choose the most appropriate area of enquiry for themselves within the context of their own knowledge and experiences. It is in this process that the teacher needs to guide on the basis of group formative evaluation coupled with an overview of the curriculum needs.

Summative – Pupil

At the completion of any project or focus of study the pupil should be encouraged to evaluate the process and the product independently of others. This evaluation could be based upon an agreed framework and helped by the informal process of formative evaluation mentioned previously. This evaluation could be measured against previous performance or within the context of the group. In most cases the pupil will proceed through a mixture of values and criteria. Some will be purely personal, others will be based upon criteria shared within the group or determined by the teacher or an examination. This type of self-evaluation will be very shallow without the knowledge and experience accumulated during previous formative evaluation activities.

Summative – Teacher

The teacher's summative evaluation or assessment of the pupils' projects should include some consideration of the pupil's ability to appraise his or her own work. This will ensure that evaluation is seen by all as an integral part of the process of art education and not as a 'bolt on activity' unrelated to the whole process.

At this stage the form and criteria of the evaluation should be clear to both pupil and teacher. On one hand it could be a recognition of the criteria embodied within the work. At the other extreme it could be an assessment against grade related criteria clearly defined at the commencement of work. Whichever method is chosen, the criteria must be clearly understood and shared between those involved.

Long Term Summative Assessment

In the final assessment of the work the process can become very complex if all options are kept open. If the summative assessment is based upon some form of examination across a complete age range of pupils, the task (long or short term) will usually be predetermined, the processes controlled and the criteria pre-set by examiners. Even when the summative assessment is based upon a collection of work over a period, the pupil should be fully aware of the criteria for any judgement. This type of open assessment will be more common in primary schools particularly with the implementation of National Curriculum. It should always be clear to everyone involved that some of the most valuable aims in art are not open to assessment. The pupils should be involved with this process because they need to understand the parameters within which they are working. The clearer they are about the overall criteria the more effectively they will be able to respond. Ideally their involvement should go beyond response and they should become personally involved with their own assessment of work. Some examinations could require pupil self-

evaluation as one of the assessable domains within the total framework.

Although examinations in the form set out above are the most common form of summative assessment they should not be seen as the only viable method. The summative assessment of work by primary teachers will be viewed in the broad context of the whole curriculum as well as within the body of knowledge called art. Secondary teachers preparing students for interviews for specialist art and design courses in colleges of F.E. and H.E. are fully aware that the summative criteria for GCSE and 'A' level may be different from one another and both are different from the criteria likely to be used in allocating places in art colleges. It is very difficult to design a range of criteria that will fulfil all academic requirements and cater for a full range of possible responses from the outrageously imaginative to the most formal technical. It can be very difficult to achieve agreement about what can, and what cannot, be assessed.

Observation of the children at work is the starting point for any evaluation or assessment. This needs to be reinforced by encouraging them to be aware of their own processes and outcomes. Through observation we can develop the critical awareness which forms the foundation for any form of judgement.

Observe infants playing constructively with bricks:

> What are they doing? Why are they doing it? What criteria are operating? Are they assessing success and failure? Are they learning from success and failure? Are they using personal judgement? Are peer group criteria operating? What is the basis for teacher intervention? Try to identify when evaluation is not taking place. How could appraisal improve the situation?

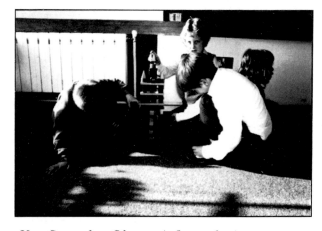

Key Stage 1 – Observe infants playing constructively with bricks.

Key Stages 2 and 3 – "The sum of our visual knowledge is not only what we know, but the way we know it and respond to it."

Key Stage 5 – Self portrait

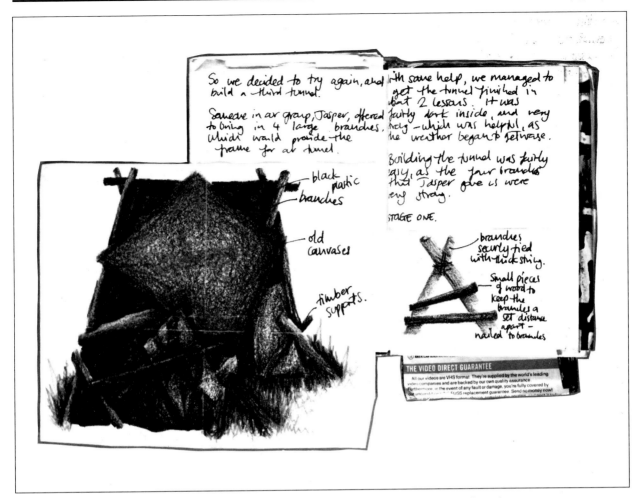

Key Stages 4/5 – Sketchbooks may be used to monitor continuous periods of work.

...............And let's face it – THEY ARE ONLY PLAYING WITH BRICKS!

Conversation with an individuals or a group is a good method of evaluating and determining what is taking place. It enables diagnosis, prognosis and development to become an integrated activity. Discussion can be the means by which the group establishes criteria which can be defined, adopted, and shared. It also allows for critical appraisal to move into a wider arena of discussing the work of other artists in the context of the pupils' own work and in the broader cultural context. Discussions can be linked with exhibitions, presentations and tutorials to provide a focus for evaluative appraisal.

Records of any self-evaluation are a good means of establishing the discipline of evaluation and assessment. It is more difficult with younger children as it requires the ability to be self aware in the context of one's own development and to be able to perceive achievements within the context of a peer group.

The advantage of self-evaluation records is that the pupil is able to look back over past activities and recognise strengths and weaknesses. They are an excellent aid to formative development.

Work Folios should be maintained in parallel with whatever form of evaluation the school has adopted. They provide positive evidence of past and current process and product. They are the essential support for both formative and summative evaluation. They are the best indicators of strengths, weaknesses and gaps in the scope of the work. It is useful to include periodically tasks which are similar such as drawings of the environment, or a colour problem, to provide a precise monitoring point. This will demonstrate to pupils and teacher the level of development and achievement over a period of time. It is an effective method to be used with younger children where self-evaluation records may not be available.

Sketch book and logs provide useful monitoring devices covering continuous periods of work. If they are dated and annotated with written notes they can form the most valuable evidence for both forms of evaluation and assessment. With younger children this could be a scrapbook for interrelated visual and verbal work.

A pupil's record of work may be useful to foster self-evaluation and link the collection of work and sketch books. These can start as a simple record of work carried out with details about the nature of the work. As the pupils become familiar with the process they could then be encouraged, with or without the teacher's assistance, to make a critical appraisal of what they are doing. This will also provide evidence of the development of their critical faculty. To assist this process a simple report form could be designed to provide a set of appropriate questions to give a shape to their responses. After factual details of the work have been completed pupils could be asked "How well do you think you have done?"; "Is your work more or less successful than last time?"; "Why?"; "What caused you greatest difficulty?"; "What part of the process appeared most useful?"; "Where are your strengths?"; "Where are you most in need of help?".

If a proforma for an evaluation is needed, it should not be too long or difficult to understand or respond to. It should also be a part of the work, i.e. used before, during and after the work. Over the years the accumulated record of evaluation would be of considerable help to pupils and teachers in designing appropriate strategies for the future, and as evidence of the development of critical self-appraisal.

Group critical sessions have to be sensitively handled to ensure the sharing of subjective judgement. Open ended questions will prompt children and enable them to participate without fear or inhibitions. In the final analysis there can never be a total consensus about the variables which enrich the whole process of artistic and aesthetic education. In any group discussion concerned with the appraisal of artwork there will always be the divergent effects of subjective and objective evaluation. These can only be resolved through a willingness to establish and share criteria which will inevitably move towards objective criteria. The sharing of subjective responses, whilst interesting and enlightening, cannot form the basis for assessment. Their main value is in enabling the

pupils and teacher recognise where they are coming from. The embodied significance of the work may be partially revealed through an understanding of the subjective values of the pupil, but art seen within the context of culture requires a recognition of shared criteria.

Group critical sessions may also expose the differences between the cognitive and affective aspects of evaluation. Some students may be concerned more about the "meaning" of the content, or the technical process, or the level of skill, whilst others may show a greater interest in the cultural aspects. Group discussions can increase the understanding of the potentially complex process. This is concerned with the ability of art to be approached from a wide range of viewpoints enabling an infinite range of responses.

These sessions can also enable pupils and students to explore the relationship between the inner reality of the artist and the social/cultural reality. Pupils will need to understand how these realities impinge upon one another in order to clarify how the criteria become embodied within the work. The differences between these and other issues will tax and enrich the group's dialogue and lead to deeper understanding, but in the end each teacher will negotiate a strategy which will enhance the educational, aesthetic and artistic value for any particular individual, group or particular area of learning.

Marking systems and examinations are the most formal forms of assessment. In most cases the task, process and criteria are prescribed for the pupil. In this type of activity the evaluation and assessment are in the control of the teacher, usually for the benefit of the institution, in the context of the broader community.

The pupils' function in this strategy is to have a clear understanding of the aims, objectives, processes, content and criteria so that they are able to make appropriate responses to fit the curriculum teaching model. Any self-assessment will have to operate within the framework prescribed by the system. Evaluation outside the set framework can still be of personal value in self directed activity, but it may not be recognised as relevant in terms of comparative assessment within the framework of grade related criteria. Any assessment objectives or attainment targets for art must be kept as open and flexible as possible within an acceptable level of shared criteria.

Activities which prescribe task, process and criteria within limited parameters run the risk of destroying that which they set out to assess. Veronica Treacher in "Assessment and Evaluation in the Arts [4]" says:

"From the outside, the teachers expressed aversions to grades, marks, grids and checklists as reliable means of summarising achievement in the arts. As the research proceeded, their reasons and valid approaches were explored. The consensus was that grading, norm referencing, rank ordering and national criteria were all deficient in describing the processes and products of children's art making. But accountability....was not to be abandoned in the face of difficulty. It should not mean examinability."

The original version of this paper by M. Barrett, was published in JADE, 1990 [7].

The Teachers' Discussions

Having been involved in discussons and practical activities relating to evaluation and assessment the teachers were grouped into their particular phase of education and were asked to respond to relevant issues.

KEY STAGE 1. 5 – 7 YEARS

We have considered the criteria for Evaluation/Assessment in relation to the process model for art, see page 13.

Considerations prior to Assessment and Evaluation

a) At what stage of development is the pupil now?

b) What does the pupil know and what is the teacher's response to that knowledge?

c) From which stage has the child come and how easy was the journey?

d) Where do we want the pupil to be and how do we help in getting the pupil there?

e) What do we expect the pupil to learn?

f) How can the pupil's cognitive understanding be developed?

g) How can we help the pupil to become more divergent and intuitive?

Considerations when evaluating work with pupils

1) Every question must be sensitively asked so no pupil ever feels threatened.

2) Initially the questions should be neutral. They must be open-ended, purposeful and thought provoking.

3) The vocabulary must be at a level that the pupil understands and vary according to the ability and experience of the pupil.

4) Care should be taken when listening to the pupil and in deciphering what the pupil is saying.

5) Some young children can display needs that are not immediately obvious. The teacher may need to probe to discover the pupil's needs and intentions.

6) The questions asked during formative assessment could form the basis of the summative evaluation.

7) The pupil must be given time to reflect and to consider answers. Timid pupils may not be able to demonstrate their views.

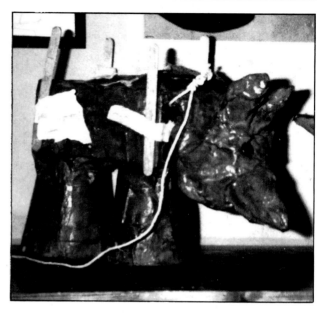

Key Stage 1 – "Sometimes I got fed up with it when I got all wet and sticky. I liked putting it together. I liked the painting but I loved covering it with the plastic glue. I would like to find a way to do less pasting."

Key Stage 1 – "I started with the hair. The face was difficult because it was too small, so I put a bit more hair on. Had trouble with the hat because the hair was too big."

8) There must be a link between verbal and visual language. The teacher must be in direct contact with the process otherwise it is impossible to make accurate comments.

9) A systematic method of questioning must be devised otherwise there will be a distorted view of the pupil.

10) The evaluation should take the form of natural conversation and should be an enjoyable social experience for the teacher and pupil.

11) The purpose of evaluation is diagnostic as well as confirmatory.

12) Both the teacher and pupil should understand the criteria being used for assessment and evaluation.

Effective evaluation can be achieved on the basis of continued observation and discussion between the teacher and the pupil. Teachers can collect their evidence while the pupil pursues a piece of work. The teacher will consider the attitude displayed as the pupil encountered various problems. The teacher must then decide whether the pupil has been resourceful, discriminating, visually aware, unique in approach, and confident in handling materials. Consideration must also be given to how the pupils managed their time, space, equipment and other pupils. Subjective evaluation of artwork is essential by both the pupil and the teacher.

Considerations for the teacher

1) Evaluation may be subjective but consideration must be given to educational objectives.

2) There must be continuous formative evaluation of the concepts, procedures and criteria. For the teacher to be successful, sensitivity towards the pupil and the criteria being evaluated must be developed.

3) The teacher has to decide whether the pupil has accepted and responded to a challenge and how the piece of work has been enriched.

4) The teacher has to decide to what extent the pupil has developed a discriminating eye and what processes were adopted while the pupil was searching for a solution to a problem.

5) Consideration must be given to how much thought, tension and frustration was evident in the process.

6) How far did the child project, predict, report, enquire, logically sort and justify the work?

7) The subject matter must be appropriate to the pupil and to the class and should stem from the pupil's personal experience.

8) Consideration must be given to what pupils have learnt.

Assessment must be based on criteria specific to the individual pupil. Summative evaluation should include the pupil's self-evaluation, which may need to be recorded by the teacher. There must be some form of written evaluation by the teacher and each school will need to adopt a uniform method of recording the evaluation.

Formative class evaluation for pupils 5-7 years could take the form of various class books with each pupil contributing one or more pages per term. Where possible the pupils should mount their own work and the class books must be relevant, worthwhile and a record of work covered. The summative evaluation would take place at the end of the school year.

Individual portfolios could be the means of evaluating each pupil's developmental progress. Individual topic books could be made and photographs taken of some 3D work. The books would provide evidence that pupils had experienced a variety of work and would indicate how their ideas, techniques, perceptions of visual form had blossomed. The problem of storage is not insurmountable. For an accurate overall assessment of the pupil it is necessary for samples of work to be kept from the day the pupil enters school, until the day school is left. Evidence of assessment and work will enable the following key stage plan for progression.

KEY STAGE 2.   7 – 11 YEARS

Considerations prior to assessing and evaluating pupils' work

Assessment and evaluation is an integral part of the making of art. It must be incorporated into the planning, the process and the outcome.

Negotiations between child and teacher play an important part in evaluation, which will be predominantly verbal and appropriate to the pupil's developmental stage. This process will involve observing, listening, talking, questioning and discussing. It may sometimes be recorded in the form of diaries or proformas attached to folio samples. The simplest record is a selection of the work of a pupil.

Formative evaluation may involve the pupil and the teacher, the pupil and a peer, the teacher and a group or class.

Considerations when evaluating the work with pupils

This list of criteria against which teachers and pupils might evaluate their work is neither exclusive nor exhaustive. It is intended to be used formatively and summatively by teachers and pupils. It begins as soon as the teachers talk to the pupil. It takes place while the work is ongoing and at the end of the work, when it may take the form of a group summative evaluation. Individual summative evaluation will involve consideration of the contents of the portfolio.

Teachers might use this evidence to build up a profile of a pupil and to plan work which ensures experience in each of the three areas of art shown in the conceptual element of the process model. (see page 13.)

Pupils could use the criteria, presented less formally, to talk about their work to the teacher

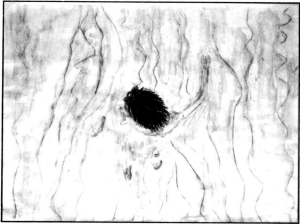

Key Stage 2 – The work of David Hockney was used to support and extend pupils' responses.

or to friends. The criteria might also help them explore their own ideas as they work. The list might also help teachers checking on a term's or a year's work to summarise for a class or an individual. After each criteria, we have framed, where appropriate, a simple question as an example of how the teacher may proceed.

Ideas, Impulses and Feelings

Is the pupil stimulated by direct personal experience and recall to make a response and express an idea visually?

Q. Where did your ideas for the water come from?
A.1. "Pulling the toy boat through the paddling pool and watching the ripples."
 2. "Seeing how people looked in the water at the pool."

Does the pupil choose the appropriate media to express ideas?
Q. Why did you choose paint/aquarelle pencil?
A.1. "I could make small strong coloured waves with the paint brush."
 2. "You can see through the colour."

Does the pupil have a personal intention for the drawing or model?
Q. What are you trying to show about the water?
A.1. "How the water moves away from the swimmer."
 2. "How the bits under water look different."

Does the pupil understand pattern and making patterns of marks?
Q. Is there any pattern developing in your picture?
A.1. "There is a pattern in the way the ripples are sort of lined up."
 2. "There is no real pattern that is repeated here."

Does the pupil explore the use of colour to express ideas?
Q. Why have you used these colours for the water?
A.1. "It wasn't really purple, but it was lots of blues."
 2. "Swimming pool water is lighter and darker blues but it is still see through."

Q. Do the colours show what you saw?

A.1. "I might have made the colours a bit brighter than they really were at the pool."

2. "Yes. It looked just like that."

Q. Do the colours show what you liked about the pool?

A.1. "Yes. It is bright and glittery and very colourful."

2. "Yes. The water is all pale and soft and calm."

Does the pupil consider the success of the work and make judgements in relation to observations and ideas?

Q. Have you enjoyed this work? Did it turn out as you wanted it to?

A.1. "Yes, but I didn't get the patterns on the water quite right, they look a bit stiff."

2. "It really looks as if he is in the water, but his leg is a bit of a funny shape."

Media, Materials and Techniques

In this area, observing and listening to pupils as they are working will provide evidence of achievement for the teacher. Questions may help the pupils' personal exploration and discovery.

Has the pupil control over a range of mark and model making materials?

Can the pupil control a range of tools and use them safely and appropriately?

Does the pupil use knowledge of the properties of materials to make an appropriate selection? Does the pupil know and use a range of joining techniques?

Does the pupil know that colours combine to make other colours?
- *know that colours can be opaque or translucent?*
- *know that the tone of colours can be changed?*

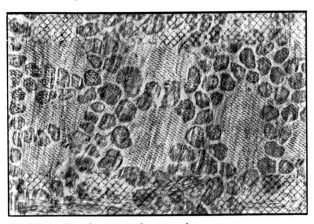

Rubbing has been used to explore texture.

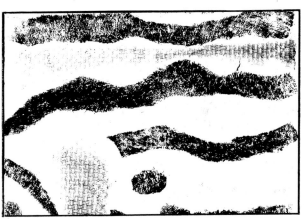

Printing is used to represent observed textures.

Clay has been used to explore forms and express ideas.

Clay has been used to explore space and form (all Key Stage 2).

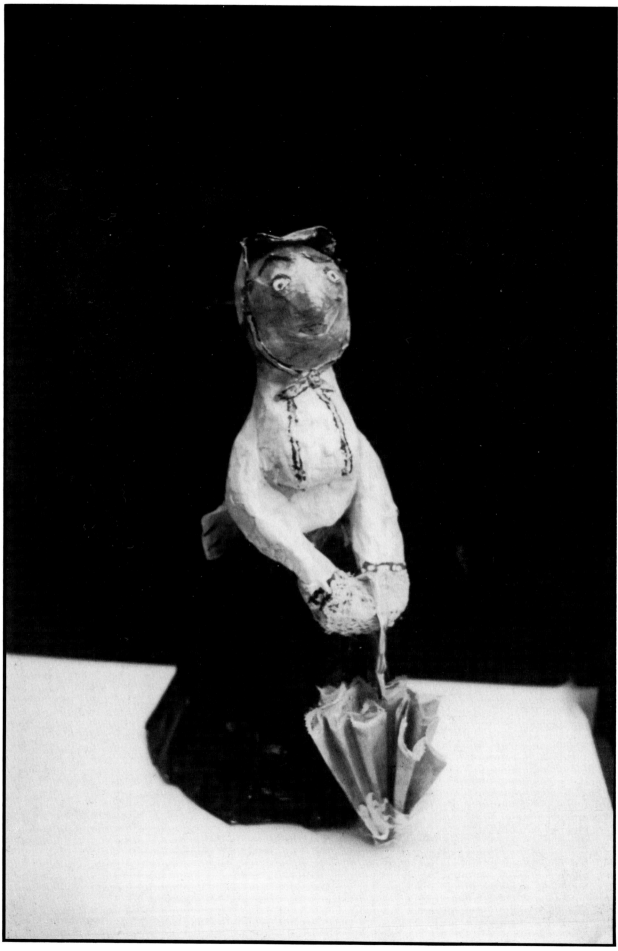

Key Stage 2 – Paper and paste figure.

Key Stage 2 – Marks are combined to represent observed shapes and spaces.

Perception of form: line, colour, texture, tone, form

Does the pupil control the elements of visual language to draw and model from observation, memory and imagination? Does the pupil use a spatial strategy appropriate to the stage of development and the subject matter of the drawing? (It may be helpful to refer to Guidelines 5-18, p.76 – 81, (24) for developmental stages.)

Does the pupil use colour with increasing subtlety in relation to observation?

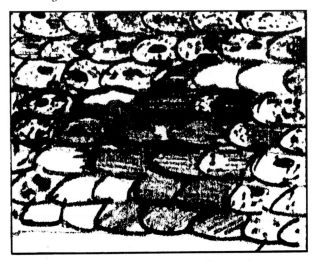

Key Stage 2 – Marks represent observed textures.

Does the pupil use marks to represent texture in relation to visual and tactile observations?

Does the pupil combine marks to represent observed and imagined shapes and spaces?

KEY STAGE 3.   11 – 14 YEARS

Evaluation starts when the first word or mark is made. It is an integral part of teaching. Sensitivity to the pupil demands confidence. Teachers need the confidence to allow the pupil to identify their route and direct themselves within a curriculum framework. This confidence can be achieved through a balance between a clear understanding of the pupil's needs, arrived at through evaluation with the pupil, and that which the teacher has planned for in terms of skills and knowledge.

If evaluation is to be a positive and constructive tool for learning and good practice teachers need to know their rationale, procedures and criteria, and to recognise the means by which the pupils may enter their work through ideas, impulses and feelings, perception of visual form, media, materials and techniques.

Consideration prior to Evaluation and Assessment

Can we identify the evaluative process in our day to day teaching?

Do we listen before asking our own questions?

Do we actually allow the pupils time to respond?

Are our questions/comments relevant and appropriate to where the pupil is?

To what extent do we determine the pupils' responses by the nature of our questions and comments?

Are our questions neutral and open ended enough?

Do we provide an opportunity for the pupil to reflect and expand?

Do we use the evidence to develop learning and teaching strategies?

How do we monitor the evidence of progression?

Are the pupils aware of the purpose of the work?

Do the pupils understand the difference between personal and group criteria?

Do we clarify subjective and objective evaluation?

Are the pupils able, as a result of evaluation to assess their work?

Do we accommodate the planned objectives and personal responses within the evaluation?

Do we plan time for evaluation?

Considerations when assessing and evaluating with pupils

How do we respond to:

I can't do it!	It's great!
It's no good!	Can I keep it?
I don't like it!	It is better than I
Can I start again?	thought it would be!
Is it alright?	It's alright now!
I'm bored!	I am pleased with it!
Do we have to?	It's not bad!
Is this what you	She is good at art!
mean?	His is good!
I don't get it!	That bit is OK!
We're not doing	
that again!	

These comments are not only an indication that help is needed but are part of the evaluative process. The teacher's response to questions should be in tune with the individual's need and allow the individual to identify a route which can be pursued. The pupil's need may arise from a lack of confidence, skills, motivation, understanding or interest.

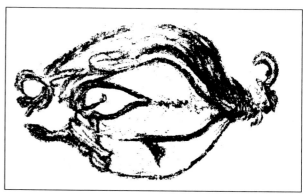

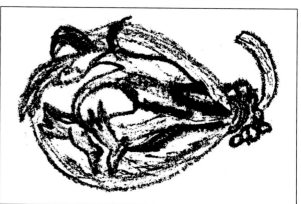

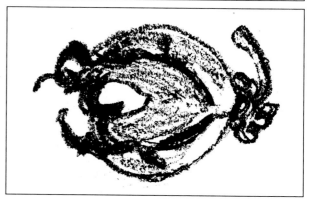

Key Stage 3 – "Why did you choose this seedpod?"

Questions should encourage dialogue and participation:

Why did you lay the boot on its side? Can you describe it to me? What did you like about that? What colour might you need? What do you like about your friend's work? Why did you choose seeds? How long have you to complete the work? What interests you about this particular issue?

We have to take account of the personal considerations which will affect their work. Individual evaluation will necessitate a different set of questions and target setting from a group evaluation.

Considerations for the teacher

Short term formative evaluation will involve the teacher in observing and listening to pupils at work and in discussion with them. This will identify the pupil's starting point, where the pupil wants to be and how this will be achieved. A diary or log/sketch book may be used to record this information. The diary may include personal comments, sketches, home-work and a collection of relevant material. This written dialogue between the teacher and pupil helps to reinforce the evaluation which has taken place within the lesson. This, in real terms, is crucial to learning outcomes.

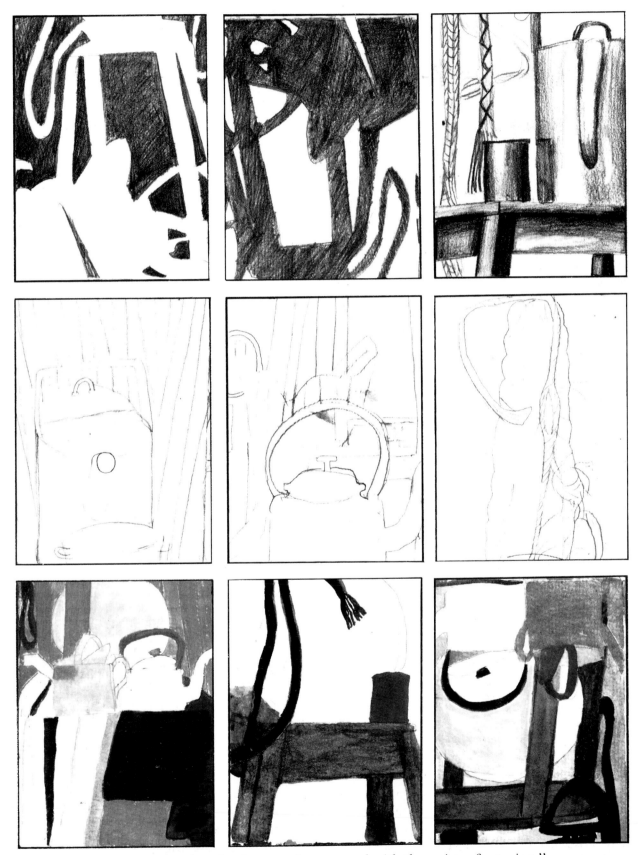

Key Stage 3 – "Longer term evaluation may be concerned with the review of a project."

Key Stage 3 – The final work will be evaluated alongside the studies, evaluation and pupils notes.

Its advantages are: beneficial training is gained by pupils in thoughtful personal evaluation; the pupil receives continuous communication and motivation; the building of a 'bank' of personal information provides a constructive source of reference for formative and summative processes; it provides an inbuilt opportunity for the teacher to detect needs and interests which did not appear apparent in the lesson.

Its disadvantages are: it demands total commitment to the time consuming task of reviewing log books regularly; ensuring accessibility of full expression for those pupils who experience difficulties with traditional forms of communication.

Longer term evaluation may be concerned with the review of a project. Upon the completion of a project a personal review may be made which may take place before or after a group evaluation. The group evaluation establishes the criteria which relate to the specified objectives. It establishes the value of personal responses, differences, comparison, attitudes, motivation, ideas, skills and media. If we are educating and not instructing, pupils will value their own responses, according to the known and accepted criteria. This in turn will grow and develop into an understanding of objective evaluation.

Formative reviews need a response from the teacher. This has a dual purpose of confirming the value of the process and considering strategies for further development. If the formative is fundamental to teaching strategy, the summative will evolve naturally and easily. It is a direct response and summary of the formative. The school will place its demands upon the summative review, and levels of achievement may need to be indicated. Information for parents may need to include interpretation of these levels, and the pupil's examination potential. Throughout these stages of evaluation it is vital that a selection of the pupil's work is stored as evidence. The pupils will have negotiated which work they wish to store. This may be kept in a personal portfolio, together with log book, sketch book and reviews. Monitoring of stored work through constant negotiation allows ownership to be a reality and contributes to meaningful evaluation and assessment.

Consideration of the process of Formative or Summative Evaluation and Assessment

Formulative evaluation – pupil/teacher, informal, ongoing

Evaluation is the central core of the teaching strategy based on one to one negotiation of meaning and need.

WHY – the purpose of such evaluation is to enable the pupils to reflect on their work so far, and to identify how it should proceed.

WHEN – it takes place during the development of a piece of work;
– it may be initiated by pupils seeking help or by the teacher touring the class.

HOW – this evaluation is done by careful neutral questioning by the teacher.

CAUTION – the teacher must avoid the trap of giving an instant solution to a perceived 'problem'.

CONSEQUENCES – pupils continue to develop their work with increased confidence and sense of purpose.

Formulative evaluation – group/teacher, informal, ongoing

Evaluation of the whole class and the teaching strategy is based upon the teacher's view of the group's collective need and derived from an evaluation of the group's responses.

WHY – its purpose is to identify changing group needs.

Key Stage 3 – Formative evaluation will enable the pupils to reflect on their work so far and to identify how it should proceed.

WHEN – it may be made internally as the teacher monitors the progress of classwork over a period, but it needs to be externalised and shared by the whole class at significant points during the progress of the work.

HOW – in the teacher's head, but shared with the group as appropriate.

CAUTION – it may challenge the teacher's original assumptions about the nature of the work initiated;
– this is the most difficult kind of evaluation as it questions teacher's strategies rather than pupil's performance.

CONSEQUENCES – it may result in a change of emphasis which is closer to the needs of the learning experience.

Formulative evaluation – pupil/teacher, more formal, periodic

Evaluation which is based upon a longer period of process and evidence, giving a wider view of pupils' longer term responses and needs.

WHY – its purpose is to enable pupil and teacher to reflect on what has been achieved and to identify areas for further development i.e. it is diagnostic.

WHEN – it takes place on completion of a whole 'project' or series of work.

HOW – it may be recorded by pupils and teachers as an aid to longer term summative evaluation;
– if a written record is made, the format should be flexible enough to allow pupils to record all that they wish to say.

CAUTION – questions should be non-judgemental whilst providing a stimulus to objective consideration;
– adequate time must be provided within lessons for this evaluation to be carried out purposefully.

CONSEQUENCES – such evaluation promotes the development of reflection and critical awareness it also provides information for parents and form tutors about the pupil's current position.

Summative evaluation – group/teacher, informal, periodic

This is a broad summation of the collective effectiveness of the joint learning strategies.

WHY – this is both formative and summative – formative in the sense that it identifies future needs, summative in the sense that it is the evaluation of completed work; group discussion helps individuals to develop some objectivity in critical awareness and to develop an appropriate language with which to express their responses; insights gained through group evaluation informs the individual's evaluation; it is important for teachers to record the effectiveness of each strategy used with each teaching group at regular intervals in order to help improve their own plans as well as keeping colleagues informed.

WHEN – on completion of a project, and carried out by the whole group;
– it may be helpful to carry out a 'group evaluation' prior to the self-evaluation.

HOW – it takes the form of a group 'critique', involving all pupils discussing all the work;
– the criteria for evaluation are to be identified within the work, both in its purpose and nature.

CAUTION – although the purpose of the work will be common to all, individuals' criteria for evaluation must also be acknowledged.

CONSEQUENCES – as we gain experience, so does our ability to provide more valuable experiences for our pupils. Any evaluation of a particular course of study will provide clues for future strategies; records of such evaluation may be kept within departments' schemes of work.

Summative evaluation – pupil/teacher, formal, periodic

This is an individual summative evaluation 'summing up' the quality of the collective process and artefact.

WHY – the school may demand some kind of norm-referenced reporting, whereas most art departments prefer to relate pupils' achievements to their own levels of ability and their own rates of progress.

WHEN – these may be required half yearly or annually; pupils and teacher complete a proforma during lesson time.

HOW – it must be a summary of formative evaluation; art departments will find ways of linking their own methods of recording to the school's system.

CAUTION – within art departments teachers must agree on common language to describe levels of achievement and must agree on a common interpretation of these levels. The language used for evaluation must be understood by pupils and parents. It is important that pupils are involved with this evaluation process, both formative and summative.

CONSEQUENCES – this system provides a general overview of pupil's progress for pupils, parents and the school.

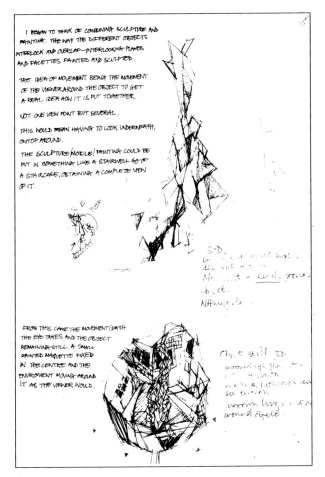

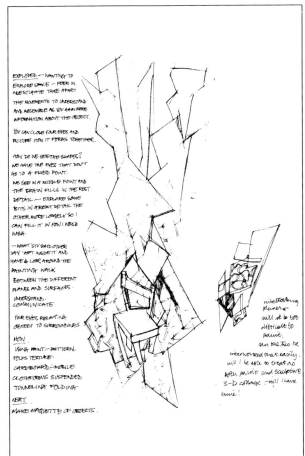

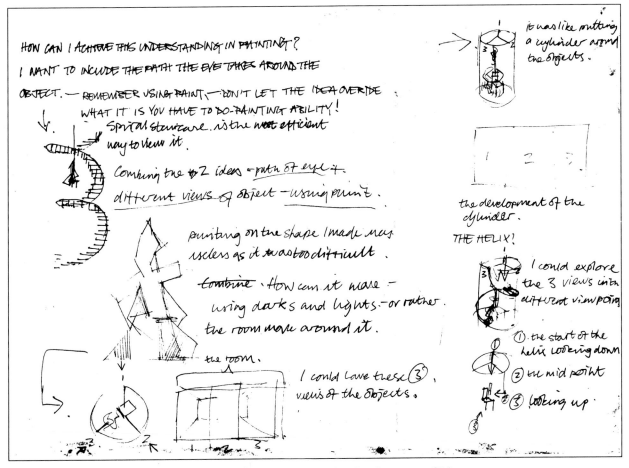

Key Stage 4/5 – Pupils' self-evaluation is integral to the development of ideas.

Key Stage 4/5 – Exhibitions provide an excellent opportunity to reflect, evaluate and assess work.

KEY STAGE 4/5. 14 – 18 YEARS

Considerations prior to Assessment

We asked questions which related to our teaching experiences within this age range in order to form a conceptual framework to assist our understanding of both formative and summative evaluation and assessment:

WHY do we assess?

WHEN do we assess or evaluate pupils' work?

HOW do we assess or evaluate pupils' work i.e. by which methods?

WHAT are we trying to assess or evaluate in pupils' work?

We defined five contexts in which assessment and evaluation takes place:

OUTSET – at the beginning of a course.

ON-GOING – day to day routine.

OUTCOME – end of project, unit, course, examination.

Key Stage 5 – Exhibited examination work.

Key Stage 1 – A carefully led multi-sensory investigation enabled the pupil to understand the qualities of the pineapple.

Key stage 4 – The medium of collage has extended exploration of the visual language.

REFLECTION – a formal review of pupil progress.

TRANSITION – re-appraisal of the pupil's past experiences in terms of their future plans.

Within the five contexts we attempted to outline the ways that evaluation and assessment may be considered at each point of the course.

Consideration of the process of evaluation and assessment

OUTSET
At the beginning of a course
Informal dialogue over work –
individual/group definition of terms
Criticism – group presentation

ONGOING
Day to day routine
Informal dialogue over work –
individual/group
Formal discussion, questions – group criticism
Review of sketchbook, log, diary,
One to one tutorial
Evaluation sheet

OUTCOME
End of project, unit or course examination
Self-evaluation sheet
Group presentation and criticism
Individual tutorial and criticism
Sketchbook/log appraisal
Marking-devised internal system
-established external system
GCSE Assessment Profile Exhibition

Key Stage 5 – Exhibited examination work.

REFLECTION
A formal review of progress
One to one tutorial
Self-evaluation
Teacher evaluation
Portfolio/sketchbook/ logbook
Exhibition, individual or group
External assessment by teacher/moderator
Record/profile/review sheet to comply with school or college needs

TRANSITION
A re-appraisal of pupil's past experiences, in terms of their future plans
Written statement regarding a student's ability and aptitude
Interview preparation, portfolio tutorial.

When reviewing work either formally or informally criteria from the lists on page 34 will be appropriate. Assessment and evaluation in a wider content may be requirements for the school or college which may have broad criteria for consideration. Consideration of the pupils' work over a period of time may show that the checklist criteria can be identified under these headings. Many will be found to apply to more than one heading:

Practical experience

comment upon the areas of specific quality, breadth or depth of control, range of practical experience.

Development of ideas

comment upon areas of learning, recognition of the shift in thinking.

Integrity

comment upon the pupil's commitment, involvement and their ability to confront the problems they encounter.

Response to guidance

comment upon the pupils' development of their level of understanding and capacity for self-evaluation.

In each of these five contexts we devised checklists to consider pupil performance and progress. We recognise that both contexts and checklists are of a transitional and developmental nature. The checklists may be considered as interrelated. They form an accumulative structure which can enable us as teachers to make formal assessments.

OUTSET Formative	ONGOING Formative	OUTCOME Formative and Summative
ATTITUDE	ATTITUDE	ATTITUDE
EXPECTATION	EXPECTATION	EXPECTATION
PRECONCEPTIONS	PRECONCEPTIONS	PRECONCEPTIONS
ADAPTABILITY	ADAPTABILITY	ADAPTABILITY
CONFIDENCE	CONFIDENCE	CONFIDENCE
MOTIVATION	MOTIVATION	MOTIVATION
INVOLVEMENT	INVOLVEMENT	INVOLVEMENT
MATURITY	MATURITY	MATURITY
CO-OPERATION	CO-OPERATION	CO-OPERATION
	COMMITMENT	COMMITMENT
	TENACITY	TENACITY
	ORGANISATION	ORGANISATION
	SELF-DISCIPLINE	SELF-DISCIPLINE
	INTEGRITY	INTEGRITY
	INDIVIDUALITY	INDIVIDUALITY
	EXPRESSIVENESS	EXPRESSIVENESS
	APPLICATION	APPLICATION
	AMBITION	AMBITION
	EXPERIMENTATION	EXPERIMENTATION
	INTERPRETATION	INTERPRETATION
	PERCEPTION	PERCEPTION
	OBSERVATION	OBSERVATION
	UNDERSTANDING & CONTROL of process	UNDERSTANDING & CONTROL of process
		RESOLUTION of process
		UNDERSTANDING of outcome
		DESIGN SKILLS
		CRAFT SKILLS
		CRITICAL AWARENESS
		AESTHETIC

SECTION II

The Structure of Visual Language: Line, Tone, Colour, Texture, Shape and Form

by Maurice Barrett

Art and design are concerned with the use of media to give visual form to our inner and exterior experiences.

This applies to the earliest responses of young children in the scribbling stage as much as to the carefully considered responses of sixth form students. Teachers may approach visual language from different standpoints. Some hold the belief that art cannot be taught. It is by its nature a personal response which is distinctly different from the responses of other people. It is essentially idiosyncratic in its conception, in the use of media and the form in which it is visualised. In the view of these teachers the only assistance that they are able to give is to enable their pupils and students to become more skilful in the "grammar and syntax" of the visual language so that they are more able to control the means by which they give form to their ideas.

Other teachers hold that such an academic approach could inhibit the free exploration of media and form. Robert Witkin[8] says that "creative vision is virtually inhibited by learned technique". The artist within each of us needs to discover that the most appropriate visual form is already embodied within the idea, and is inseparable from it.

Whether we believe that visual form is embodied within the idea or that the idea can be enhanced through the application of a knowledge of visual form, it is useful if the teacher is able to understand the dynamics of visual sensation with particular reference to colour, shape, line, texture and structure. With this knowledge the teacher will be in a better position to help pupils understand and extend the range of possible avenues open for them to explore.

A comprehensive knowledge and understanding of the dynamics of visual language will not ensure the creation of works of art. But without some level of conscious control over the way that the artefact is structured it will lack the essential discipline which enables the idea to be embodied in an appropriate form. Teachers will have experienced the frustration of children whose lack of skill and knowledge inhibits the realisation of their ideas. Exercises which enable children to explore the affects of colour, line, tone and texture will be of limited value unless they are seen as being part of the process of giving visual reality to individual ideas and concepts. This whole theme is explored by M J Parsons in "How we understand art"[9].

Mary Warnock[10] in an essay on imagination defined it as "the ability to see more in the immediate.... than meets the immediate eye". The more we educate our eyes the keener our perceptions will become. These will consequently influence and enrich our responses. Our visual senses are educated through direct experience. The best way to explore colour is through practical manipulation of its qualities through a variety of media. Theoretically defining the relationships between primary, secondary and tertiary colours by using the colour circle is irrelevant, if the mixing of red and blue in practice does not produce the anticipated purple.

Colour exists in a wide range of media which will create a variety of results. It is through the direct exploration of different materials that pupils will discover the full potential of these variables. Crimson and cobalt will not produce the same "purple" as scarlet and ultramarine, but in crude terms they are reds and blues. The dynamics of visual form need to be experienced through the senses rather than taught as an abstract body of knowledge. The learning process needs to be explored within the context of

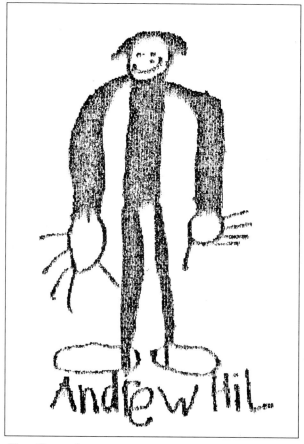

Key Stage 1

Key Stage 2

Key Stage 3

Key Stage 4

The control of visual language enables pupils to express and extend ideas, impulses and feelings.

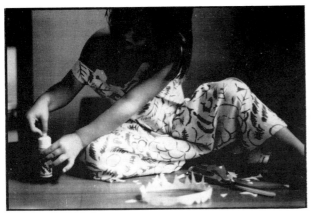

Key Stage 1

ideas rather than through abstractions. The initial ideas may be introduced through the practical manipulation of form but this should be developed within the context of the pupils' ideas, and through the manipulation of media. No rules or regulations can ever be a substitute for enlightened human insight.

It is essential to view the elements of visual form within the reflexive framework of art. They are inseparable from the use of media, materials and techniques and the conceptualisation of ideas, impulses, feelings and perceptions.

Art and aesthetics should not be confused with one another. Louis Arnaud Reid[11] described aesthetic attitudes as:

> "...when we attend to, enjoy contemplatively, anything for its own sake, for itself, for its intrinsic interestingness – and not for the sake of increasing factual or conceptual knowledge, or for practical or any other external reasons. Patterns of abstract ideas .... can be aesthetic 'objects' .... of colours, sounds, patterns of them, textures, forms of all kinds. These are, of course, included in the qualities of art, but aesthetic interest extends far beyond art to the whole realm of nature and to human constructs which are not as such art."

This clear distinction between art and aesthetic is important when dealing with the function of form in art. Art may be aesthetically appealing but not all things which appeal aesthetically are art.

Reid continues:

> "A work of art is something made with aesthetic intention .... something that can be contemplated and enjoyed for its own sake, and also something which expresses and embodies a perceived material/medium, values, ideas and meaning which could not possibly be expressed

Key Stage 3 – "The dynamics of visual form need to be experienced through the senses."

and embodied .... in any other way".

The meaning or significance of a work of art is embodied in its perceived form. Visual form without meaning can be appreciated aesthetically for its own sake in the same way as we can appreciate the pattern of a dragonfly's wing or a sunset. But the making and appreciation of art goes beyond purely aesthetic considerations.

The awareness of form occurs naturally from a very early age. Children of two years have already developed the ability to work within the implied boundaries of a sheet of paper. These "placement patterns" are the earliest evidence of their control of mark marking. The early years of scribbling demonstrate increasing dexterity, not only in the control of the mark makers but the marks themselves. Without teaching or guidance children develop increasingly complex control over marks, imbuing them with their own significance until they develop symbolic schema which will enable them to express their own responses to the objects in their world. The ordering of their marks not only enables them to respond pictorially but it can also help them to experiment

Key Stage 4

with patterns which are units or designs repeated which become predictable; and designs which are the organisation of elements into a unified whole. These terms need to be understood by the pupils so that they can differentiate between them. They discover visual patterns in nature and in human constructs, as well as in their own work, using marks, building bricks and sounds. Designs are the organisation of visual or structural elements onto a unified whole. Designs can be purely aesthetic organisations but they can also be functional as in machinery or artistic as in any work of art.

Maurice de Sausmarez[12] says that 'Basic Design' should be:

"...an attitude of mind not a method .... emphatically not an end in itself but a means of making the individual more acutely aware of the expressive resources at his (or her) command; a fostering of an inquisitiveness about phenomena .... in the external world or the interior world of visions, personal reactions and preferences".

We must not allow the exploration of what Ozenfant[13] calls "the geometry of sensation" to exclude free spontaneous gestures and unconscious impulses. We should encourage children

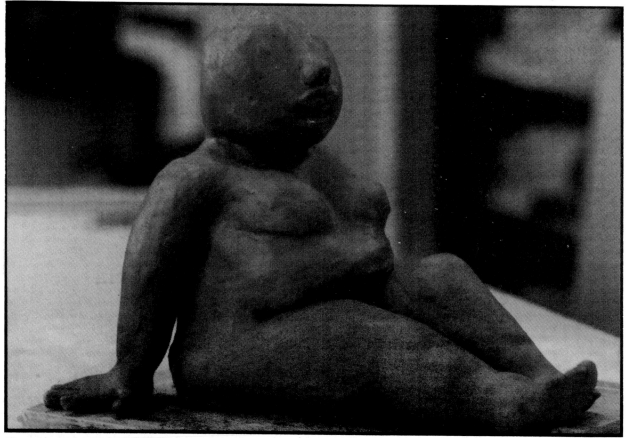

Key Stage 3 – "The elements of visual form are inseparable from the use of materials, media and techniques and the conceptualisation of ideas, impulses, feelings and perceptions."

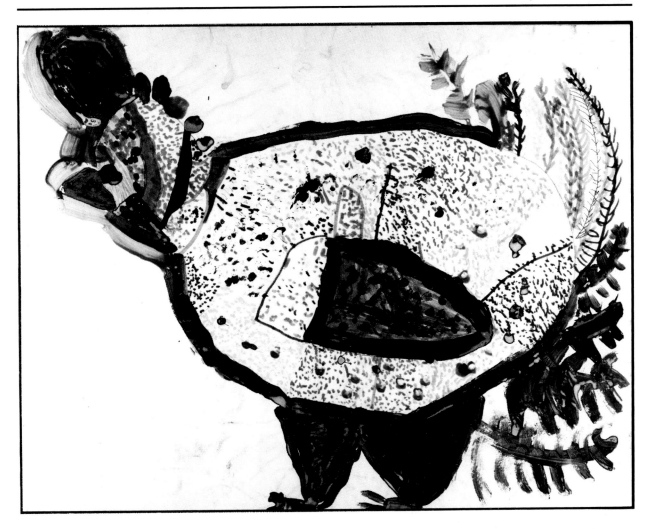

Key Stage 1 – Nursery children painting with "...free spontaneous gestures...".

Key Stage 1 – The placement of marks in colour, line and texture are the means by which pupils give visual form to their idea and perceptions.

to see that an understanding of visual form can guide decision making and assist the development of intuitive judgement. The placement of marks in colour, line and texture are the means by which they can give visual form to their ideas and perceptions.

This can be achieved most effectively by encouraging pupils to question the decisions they are making within the context of their own ideas and against a background of a developing vocabulary of visual form. In the final reckoning it is essential for the dynamics of visual form to be seen as an essential and reflexive element of art. Art cannot exist without a consideration of form. But form considered in isolation, for its own sake, can only be viewed aesthetically. David Best[14] makes this point clearly when discussing creativity:

"For it is central to the meaning of (creativity) that to be creative is, precisely to do something original which necessarily could not be achieved solely by following rules or satisfying general criteria. It is only if what is achieved transcends or even changes the rules and general criteria that it could be creative."

As always the teacher has to resolve the problem of freedom or control. Too much freedom and there is a risk of the pupils being inhibited through the lack of skills needed to realise their ideas in a visual form. Too much control through the imposition of criteria related to form and there is the risk of inhibiting the pupils' freedom to create original responses. But it is clear that within this dichotomy there must be an awareness of the part that visual language plays in the embodiment of meaning within any work of art.

The Teachers' Discussions

Having been involved with the practical activities relating to the structure of visual language, the teachers were grouped into their particular phase of education and were asked to respond to relevant questions.

KEY STAGE 1. 5 – 7 YEARS

Learning about visual language should take place within the context of class activity in and outside the classroom. All activities, such as going for a walk, gardening, cooking, investigating an old sewing machine or a doll from foreign parts offer an opportunity to explore visual dynamics. For example, contrasts in colour, size and shape and changes in texture of the flowers and trees in the garden can be investigated. Recording these experiences through drawing or modelling, gives the pupils an opportunity to explore the dynamics of visual language for themselves.

What is the appropriate range of mark markers?

The only limitations on the type of marker to be made available are wieldiness (some markers are too big or too heavy for an infant hand), safety (lino cutters would not be appropriate) and expense (aquarelle pencils are probably more sensibly kept for a later stage).

Too great a range presented at one time might prove to be a distraction and prevent the concentration that shows the pupils' natural delight in experimentation.

What type of mark making should be explored?

Marks with fingers, hands, feet and a range of implements on vertical and horizontal surfaces, ranging from pieces of paper to sand trays, walls and pavement. The quality of the mark made could be indicated by the teacher "Look you have made a trail of little marks with your feet" or "What a fat line that brush can make" and discussed with the pupils rather than attempting to guide the pupils to make marks of any particular quality.

Marks will be made in the activities of drawing, painting, printing, collage, rubbing, impression, casting, stitching, scratching and in using sand and clay.

Key Stage 1 – Line is used to enclose an area and depict details.

What are appropriate learning experiences?
Experiences which allow pupils the opportunity to explore.

Line
At this stage the pupils use line very simply to enclose an area or depict a detail. For example, an eye is enclosed and eyelashes are added. Marks are mostly used to make symbols such as the lollipop tree, rather than to draw what has been seen.

There is not often evidence of a change of quality in the line used other than that achieved by a change of media, but when pupils are making patterns or decorating pictures, different types of marks are made. Their interest in the variety of line might be fostered at this time.

Colour
Teachers should draw pupils' attention to the variety of shade and hue to be found in the natural and made world. Pupils should be given the opportunity to discover the variety of colour that can be made using different media and the effect that colour has upon us and on neighbouring objects.

Key Stage 1 – Texture is experienced through touch, sight and sound.

Pupils should be encouraged to express shapes and spaces physically. (Sculpture park by Andy Frost.)

Texture

Texture is experienced through touch, sight and sound. Pupils' attention can be drawn to the variety of texture in the natural and made world. Rubbing, impression, casting, printing, drawing and describing will help pupils understand the differences between what they can see and what they can feel. Texture can be shown in 2D work (drawing, painting, printing) by pencil or brush marks. When clay is used textures are shown by changing its surface. Collage also enables pupils to explore textures and use them to interpret observations.

Shape and Form

Pupils should be encouraged to explore physically shapes and spaces, going in and under, through and round. Comparisons can be made.

Are we looking at something two or three dimensional?

Are we looking at straight or curved edges?

Are we looking at something hollow or solid, light or heavy?

Are we looking at something symmetrical?

Can we find pattern in the shapes and forms?

KEY STAGE 2. 7 – 11 YEARS

Visual language is not a separate element to be taught in isolation, but one which needs to be considered by the teacher when developing the pupil's response to direct experience. The teacher will need to structure and plan experiences which foster curiosity about line, colour, space, tone, pattern and texture. Opportunities to do this will occur across the curriculum. Awareness of a pupil's developmental stage is vital if these experiences are to be relevant and appropriate.

The way in which line, colour, texture, tone, shape and form are used can suggest more than the eye can see. Isolated exercises may achieve "slick" results but will deny the pupil the opportunity to express their personal responses.

What is the appropriate range of mark makers?

The range of mark makers for 5-7 years continues to be appropriate for this age group.

It is important to encourage the pupils to select from a variety of mark makers. But there will be occasions when the teacher chooses to limit the choice of materials to focus the exploration.

Using a non-conventional range of mark makers such as fingers, sticks, sponges and feathers to record observations can also help the pupils focus their looking and develop visual language.

Key Stage 2 – "At this stage pupils use line to analyse what they see."

Key Stage 2 – "Learning experiences should be related to observations and relevant direct experience."

There is no limitation to the forms which may be explored other than the relevance to the child. Opportunities to plan for these experiences will occur across the whole curriculum. Suitable mark marking activities include construction in paper and paste, clay, or textiles, drawing and painting, printing, collage and montage.

What are appropriate learning experiences?

Line

At this stage pupils use line to analyse what they see. Pupils are concerned with "getting it right". Teachers must take care to discover which "right" the pupil means and not impose their own perception. To help them get it "right" teachers need to ask questions which focus on the looking and not interfere with the drawing. The focus will depend upon the purpose of the drawing. For example, is the drawing to show accurate detail, size and structure?

Colour

Pupils are interested in matching the colours they use to the world they see. Pupils need to understand through experience, how colours work in a range of materials.

Key Stage 2 – Work in 3D will give pupils an understanding of form and space.

Texture

As with pupils in key stage one, an exploration of real textures should be the basis of learning experiences. The techniques suggested for key stage one continue to be suitable. Printing, (the transference of a quality of a surface) can extend the experience.

Shape

Learning experience should be related to observations and relevant direct experience.

Pupils at this stage are rarely interested in shape for shape's sake. They are interested in the shape of things like cars, trees and people.

Links with work on shape in mathematics can be made – observing the patterns of scales of a fish, tiles of roofs, brickwork, branching trees and so on. Work on shape may support pattern and tessellation.

Form

Pupils 'earlier' physical exploration should be extended. Work in three dimensions (clay, paper and paste) will give pupils an understanding of form and space. Pupils are excited by the physical reality of 3D making which relates to the world as they experience it.

KEY STAGE 3.   11 – 14 YEARS

Pupils at this stage of adolescence will have a desire to reproduce images which are sophisticated, but as yet, the pupils are not equipped with the skills, knowledge and understanding to represent their ideas adequately. They begin to use visual language in a more considered way, provided that their attention is drawn to the variety of choices available to them. At this age they can be intrigued and stimulated by different effects created by the re-arrangement of elements within a visual structure. Their curiosity can be sustained, so that experimenting with alternatives can be undertaken with a sense of purpose and enjoyment.

Increased awareness of adults' work may create an assumption that there is an elusive 'right' way to do things, involving the manipulation of visual elements in a mystical way. There may be a demand for formulas to solve particular problems such as "How do you draw trees?". Dialogue between pupil and teacher will demonstrate that there are many choices available, rather than a single perfect solution. Any decision made will have been negotiated between teacher and pupil. It is the teacher's responsibility to enable pupils to develop the ability to make conscious decisions in using

Key Stage 3 – "Visual language is integral to the embodiment of meaning."

Key Stage 2 –
The celebration of festivals
provides opportunities to
explore ideas, materials
and techniques.

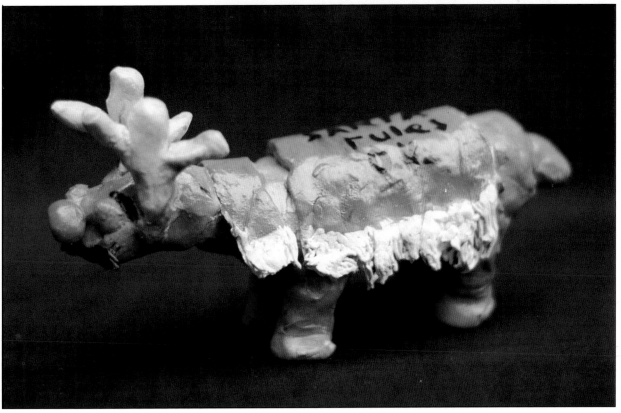

Key Stage 3 – Pupil's decisions show both an aesthetic and artistic awareness. (Lino print.)

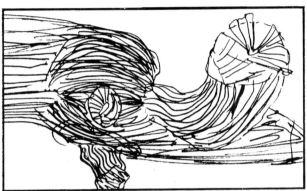

Key Stage 3 – Exploration of materials and media related to focussed looking.

Line

as line, line as tone, line as movement, line as space

Tone

as form, tone as mood, tone as part of composition tone as space, tone within colour

Shape

as representation, shapes as part of composition, organic/mechanical, emerging shapes from other shapes; positive/negative

Form

weight, structure, 3 dimensional, scale, balance, representation, form as tone, form as line, form as movement, the tactile nature of form

Colour

local, atmospheric, mixtures of colours, colour/tone/hue, harmony, contrasts, colour as element of composition, mood, colour as an element of space

Pattern

observed, designed, mathematical connections, pattern as texture, pattern as structure, and as decoration, within the natural and made world

Texture

considerations of surfaces, seen, created, felt

Space

to be manipulated within a framework, both 2 dimensionally and 3 dimensionally; emptiness and fullness and disturbed space, positive/negative.

Design

the consideration of any organisation of elements into a unified whole, e.g. a flag, a section of a tree trunk, a man hole cover.

KEY STAGE 4/5. 14 – 18 YEARS

There are many different ways of introducing and dealing with visual language at this key stage. By the end of Year 9 pupils will have been exposed to and experienced the potential of line, tone, shape, colour, pattern, texture, space, composition and aesthetic dynamics. Teachers at this level would aim to extend this experience, through a broad and flexible pro-

cess of exploration, experimentation, analysis, execution and interpretation. The emphasis is usually on a questioning of the whole concept of the dynamic language and function of visual form.

What is the appropriate range of mark markers and materials? What type of mark making or forms should be explored?

There are no limitations to the use of mark making materials in this age group other than those which might be imposed for health and safety reasons. Activities would aim to extend previous experiences. Pupils would be encouraged to explore the mark making potential of an unlimited range of implements, media and approaches. The emphasis here would be on experimentation and encouraging discovery through "doing".

What are appropriate learning experiences?

Selective activities that focus on one or more aspects of the elements of visual language. These may be skills based, open ended, technical, problem solving, theoretical, mathematical, contextual, but above all questioning and extending the potential of the individual or group.

As the students are moving through different developmental stages, teachers need to create situations that sharpen their perception of visual form in the way that is most appropriate. These may include situations which extend or develop understanding of:

colour theory
spatial dynamics
linear dynamics
tonal dynamics
compositional arrangements
elements related to perspective
the handling of materials
the static versus the active
mark making
the golden mean / section
2D space and form / 3D space and form.

Consideration of line and tone should encourage an investigative approach to linear design and an awareness of the effects of tonal

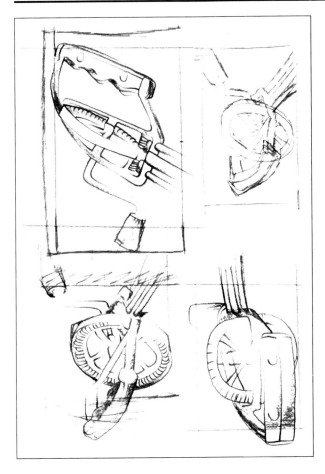
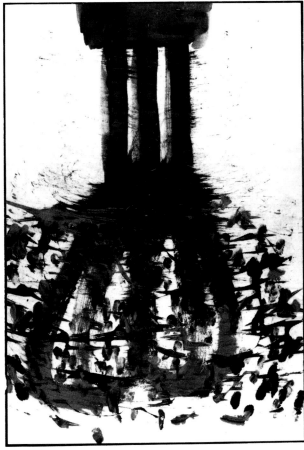

Key Stage 5 — Line and colour are used to create rhythm, movement and energy.

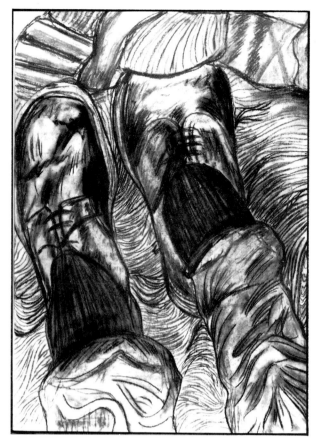

Key Stage 5 – "An awareness of the physical chracteristics of line."

Key Stage 5 – "The meaning of a piece of work is contained within the work."

design and an awareness of the effects of tonal variation and contrast.

Teachers may consider:

– the use of outline and contour as a physical compositional element and as an expressive element within an artefact;

– the use of line to create rhythm, movement, energy, volume, depth, weight;

the use of line to divide or link elements within visual form an awareness of the physical characteristics of line, smooth, rough, heavy, fast, broken;

– the use of tone to give a sense of three dimension, the illusion of volume and depth;

– the use of tone to give emphasis, a focus, contrast;

– the use of tone to give atmosphere, for example chiaroscuro in Rembrandt, George de la Tour;

– the potential of tone as an expressive element for example a spiritual light.

At these key stages we would hope that by sharing responses to the dynamic nature of visual elements within any artistic form it would encourage pupils to recognise that the meaning of a piece of work is in the end contained within the work.

SECTION III

Aesthetic Sensitivity and Critical Studies

by Maurice Barrett

Education through art, craft and design will be incomplete unless pupils and students are able to develop a critical awareness of their own work and that of others. They need to learn how to appraise things aesthetically and functionally as well as artistically. An object, environment or sensory experience can be appreciated aesthetically for its own sake. A dragonfly's wing or a sunset can foster an aesthetic response. This response may be positive or negative.

A work of art can also be appreciated aesthetically but the critical appraisal of art goes beyond this. Any work of art has a meaning embodied in its form which gives it a significance beyond purely aesthetic appreciation. Any aesthetic attention to an object or sensory experience is intrinsically and instrumentally a good preparation for the making and appreciating of art and design.

L.A.Reid[16] says:

"Art is a human making 'with aesthetic intention' and it is also a made thing to be contemplated and enjoyed."

He emphasizes the need to make a clear distinction between the two modes of appreciation:

"Aesthetic interest extends far beyond art into the whole realm of nature and to human constructs which are not, as such, art."

General aesthetic awareness can become the foundation for the appreciation of art and design, but art is more complex and concentrated:

"An artist gives visual form to ideas, impulses and feelings by mixing his (or her) mind with his (or her) materials." (Samuel Alexander)[15].

A purely aesthetic judgement is private, arising out of our sensitivity to an object or experience. Our judgement is not dependant upon the object so much as upon the nature of our personal response to it. No meaning has been embodied within the aesthetic object, whereas in art, the artist works to give meaning to the act of making. The spectator is invited to enter into it. The artist's intention is to infuse meaning into the objects or the performances created. The spectator's response is aesthetic, coupled with a search for the meaning and significance conveyed by the artist through the chosen medium of expression.

The starting point for any critical appraisal is to understand that the meaning of a work of art is embodied within its form. It is not referential, its meaning cannot be communicated adequately in another form. To develop an ability to recognise, appraise and appreciate a work of art the pupils need to develop approaches which enable them to enter into the work.

An immediate aesthetic response, an interest in the subject matter, the handling of materials and techniques, or a response to the dynamics of visual form may be the trigger for further activity. Any of these aspects could form the basis for an extension of knowledge and understanding. Whether this takes place as part of the formative development of the pupil's own work or is related to the work of a given artist or designer, the processes could develop along similar lines. Thus parallel aspects of learning would be enriched through and about, art and design.

The world is not only divided between natural and artistic objects. The most common elements in our environment are human constructions, from transistors to railways stations, from hats to jumbo jets. They can provide experiences as rich as the natural world. Teachers need to foster and extend pupils' critical faculties through continuous appraisal and

A table lamp is not a work of art in so far as it does not have a meaning embodied within it. It is structured in order to fulfil a defined function effectively. Within the maker's brief for such an object there would probably be the consideration of appropriate materials, cost, ergonomics, manufacturing processes, aesthetic form, and style.

The criteria for the functional aspect of such an object can be set out very clearly in terms of fitness for purpose, and tested in absolute or comparative terms. Aesthetic considerations will still be private and personal as described previously.

Aesthetic considerations for functional objects will not be as open as in the responses to natural objects. There will probably be some consideration of style. Style may be seen as the "way" in which the object is made or fulfils its purpose. These different "ways" can be recognised as a set or family of solutions. Subsequent designs may be developed to fit into this family of responses. In making an aesthetic judgement of such designs the styles of the object may be as

important a determining factor as the response to the object in isolation.

Ask the pupils to make judgements about the designs of a range of different teapots. Ask them to test them – functionally for pouring, holding, balance, heat retention, lid fit, and stability. Ask them to consider the teapots aesthetically in isolation, and then within the style of their own home or the school canteen or staffroom. The same activity could be structured around the design of chairs or hats.

The pupils could be asked to discuss the weight they give to functional as opposed to aesthetic criteria.

Specific Artistic Focus as a Starting Point

This is when works of art are used as a starting point to initiate particular forms of response, or lines of enquiry, and give pupils the opportunity to come into contact with the work of artists. The pupils may be shown a collection of reproductions of one artist, or group

Key Stage 3 – Pupil's observational drawing of the local environment have been supported and extended by looking at the work of the Boyle family.

Key Stage 4 – Looking at a variety of artist's landscapes has supported a pupil's particular line of enquiry. (silk screen print)

of artists, in order to focus upon a particular process or quality of work.

> *Van Gogh's landscapes could be used to explore the quality of broken colour; impasto application of paint; dynamic use of brushstrokes; the use of pure colours together to create colour mixing.*
>
> *John Piper's paintings of buildings could be used to demonstrate the textured qualities which can be achieved with wax-resist techniques (i.e. using wax crayon and over painting with thin water colours, dyes or inks).*
>
> *David Hockney's swimming pools could be used to focus upon the patterns to be found in the movement of water surfaces.*
>
> *Henry Moore's sculpture could be used to introduce pupils to the idea of penetrated and separated forms and structures.*
>
> *J.M.W.Turner's landscapes and seascapes could be used to focus upon the ideas of light and atmosphere.*
>
> *Elizabethan miniatures could be used to focus upon the use of patterns to enrich clothing.*
>
> *Claude Monet's series of paintings of Rouen Cathedral could be used to explore the colour of shadows and the changing effect of light.*

General Artistic Focus as a Starting Point

This is when pupils are presented with a range of examples to explore different responses to and interpretations of a concept, such as landscape. To expand the concept of landscape a variety of approaches could be used.

> *Examples of C15th Italian painting illustrate the use of landscape as a background. Oriental paintings show alternative approaches to space. Van Gogh, Vlaminck, Carot, Turner, Samuel Palmer demonstrate mood and 'landscape as a frame of mind'.*
>
> *To expand the concept of water, examples might be chosen from the work of Turner, Monet, Derain, Canaletto, Constable, Hockney, Kokoschka, Hokusai, and the Bayeux tapestry.*

Resourcing to Support and Extend Pupil's Work

This is where the teacher selects works of art from a bank of resources in books, reproductions, postcards and slides to support and extend work in progress. The initial motivation will come after the pupil's response to direct experience. The teacher will then try to extend the development by presenting the pupil with a range of examples of the work of artists, which may support the pupil's response or show other possible approaches.

There is also the issue of whether the works of art are seen purely as support for the pupils' own work or whether, when presenting them to pupils, they are introduced as "works of art" in a social, cultural, artistic and historical context.

Teachers might consider categorising their resources: landscapes, buildings, still life, looking through (windows – doors etc.), people, flowers, water, colour, and shape.

The Artistic Ambience of the School

This approach is less specific in operation. It is concerned with the creation of an ambience or ethos. Central to this approach is the teacher, whose interest, knowledge and resources, are used to enrich and enlighten the pupil in the continuous process of learning. It will depend upon the teacher's skill in using art, craft and design as a resource whilst deepening the pupils' understanding, awareness and sensitivity. This approach is complementary to previous approaches. It is broader in its aims and objectives and enables links to be made with other arts and the full arena of learning. It is not a structured strategy so much as the creation of an artistic ambience.

Further Considerations

Most art teachers would agree that critical appraisal is an essential part of art, craft and design education. As in other areas of the art curriculum different teachers will wish to place different emphasis in their approach to the subject. The main dichotomy is between those who would place more emphasis upon the process of education through the practice of art and others who believe that, by working from an understanding of the nature and range of the work of artists, the pupils' own work will be enriched and extended. The former approach moves towards an understanding of cultural and artistic values. The teachers will work from the premise that by immersing children in their own practical, expressive, aesthetic and artistic

Key Stage 5 – "Using the work of Italian futurists to resource, support and extend the pupils' work."

Displays of natural and made objects stimulate aesthetic sensitivity.

activities they will be more able to recognise the nature and significance of the work of others. In the latter approach it is hoped that the richness, variety and intensity to be found in the work of artists, past and present, will

Key Stage 3 – "What about popular culture."

inspire and illuminate the way children approach their own artistic endeavours.

In all matters related to art education a broad diversity of approaches will send the message to children that their art is enriched by open minded flexibility. Teachers will continue to decide upon the most appropriate strategy within the context of their own knowledge, experience, interests and resources.

Teachers might like to consider the following questions before deciding upon appropriate strategies:

– does the teacher need to know about art?
– does this knowledge have to be culturally diverse?
– are some works of art more relevant to specific phases of education?
– does a knowledge of art enrich and extend the pupils' practical activities?
– do we mean "high culture" when we talk about art? What about popular culture? The vernacular craft tradition? Ethnic diversity? Style? Fashion?
– are we using art for aesthetic or practical education?
– what is the best way to confront children with art, craft and design?
– how far are pupils in each key stage able to develop criteria beyond the skilful representation of beautiful reality?

The Teachers' Discussions

Having been involved in discussions, the teachers were then grouped into their particular phase of education and were asked to respond to relevant questions.

KEY STAGE 1.   5 – 7 YEARS

What aesthetic experiences are appropriate when considering the natural world?

In this phase pupils should be encouraged to share and focus on their experiences of natural objects and events within their environment. Their aesthetic learning is all about their own responses to sensory experiences. It is how children feel and react when they touch, smell, hear or taste. Sometimes they will like the experience, but maybe they will not. Young pupils should be given opportunity and time to describe these experiences and allow their sensory feelings to grow.

What experiences and activities are appropriate?

The children could make personal and class collections of found and natural objects to handle, examine, sort and discuss. Conkers, feathers, leaves, stones, fruits or seeds, which have been gathered for science activities can provide aesthetic experiences. Teachers should help pupils capture that magic of the moment when a rainbow is spotted, the hailstones bounce off the roof, the dry leaves are crunched underfoot or the wind blows through their hair. Activities like guess the smell, meet and hug a tree, look at the sky and treetops through a mirror on the ground or arrange a pile of stones, will help to focus attention. Using looking devices like hand lenses, viewfinders, reflectors and microscopes will help pupils see in more detail. Asking questions such as "Why did you choose that one?" and "What did you like about it?"

"Aesthetic learning is about pupils' response to sensory experiences of natural and made objects."

will help pupils understand their own responses.

What aesthetic learning is appropriate when considering functional design?

Just like the learning from natural objects, it is the pupils' personal experience of human structures and artefacts that matter. Pupils should have opportunity to play with a wide range of functional objects such as toys, and explore environments such as the playground. They should be encouraged to express their ideas and feelings about these things and places. Questioning should be open-ended so that replies such as "This is a good car because it goes fast", or "I don't like the playground because it is crowded" would come naturally.

What learning experiences and activities are appropriate?

Handling, describing, comparing, sorting, classifying, questioning and experimenting are some of the ways in which pupils can see whether an object works. They can consider the suitability of the design through questions like "Will it look nice in the dolls house?", or test function when prompted with a question like "Is the chair strong enough to sit on?". Again pupils should be given time to consider, ponder and reflect, organise and express their thoughts.

What aesthetic learning is appropriate when considering art and craft?

Pupils develop ideas and discover the form of things from their own experiences. However, it

Key Stage 1 – "Critical awareness will start with evaluation, discussion and display of pupils' own work."

is often relevant for pupils to enjoy the work of other artists and craftworkers. Illustrations in story books, puppets and masks, animal carving, reproductions of paintings and prints can be interesting components of work in many areas of the curriculum.

Pupils need to see works of art and craft so that they understand that adults enjoy working in this way as well as children. At this stage lines between aesthetic responses, 'craft', 'functional design' and 'art' will be blurred, but the distinction can begin to be made between "Does it look nice?" and Does it work?" and "Do you think the artist liked the woods he has painted?".

It will be a pity if children only ever see reproductions of other people's work. Original works might be borrowed from local secondary schools, sixth form college or a local art society. An artist might come to the school to work with the children.

What learning experiences and activities are appropriate?

In the school environment the first art which infants will become aware of will be their own and that of their peers. Critical awareness could well start with evaluation, discussion and a display of their own work. A walk around the school occasionally, to see what other classes have been doing, or a few minutes spent in the hall after assembly to examine the work of another class could be a beginning.

Pupils can be introduced to the work of artists outside the school, in the context of the whole curriculum. When the pupils are thinking about families, reproductions of paintings of family, portraits from the past and present

Key Stage 1 – "Pupils need to see works of art and craft so that they understand that adults enjoy working in this way as well as children."

might be displayed with the photographs the pupils bring from home, and find in magazines. When they are making a colour collection, the work of artists or craftworkers might be included.

To stimulate and develop ideas pupils might be introduced to the work of other artists and craftworkers. For example embroideries and applique work from South America might be shown to them when they are working with stitches or with fabric collage. At Christmas they might see the way that other artists have painted the story of the nativity. A variety of crib figures might be displayed. What is important is that variety is shown, so that the children begin to understand that there are many ways to express the same idea.

It is unlikely with infants, that the teacher will find the opportunity to suggest that pupils think about another artist's work while they are actively involved in their own. However, when the pupils have finished their work there is opportunity to introduce the work of other artists. When the pupils have painted a rabbit they might be interested to see some animal pictures. When they have drawn some flowers they might like to see other flower pictures.

It is very important that pupils are not encouraged to copy other people's work which will almost certainly be inappropriate to their own stage of development.

The Ambience of the School
A school building can provide a visually rich and stimulating environment which arouses curiosity, asks questions, accepts contributions and offers possibilities. It will reflect the school's learning policy and accommodate the individuality of the school. To create this ambience demands time and commitment. Used as a tool for learning it will support pupils' ability to be observant and critical.

KEY STAGE 2. 7 – 11 years

When considering the natural and made world, what experiences are appropriate to develop an aesthetic and critical awareness?
Pupils should be provided with time and opportunities for direct sensory experiences of the natural world. Thoughts and feelings will be developed through sharing these experiences by comparing, reflecting and discussing.

Environmental studies could include sensory walks in the school grounds, in woods and by ponds. Looking can be focused in some novel ways. "Ant hills" help pupils explore a small patch of ground very closely. Samples of natural materials can be organised to make "rainbow chips". Asking pupils to choose personal places for reflection will encourage analysis and decision making. The swimming pool provides opportunities to observe distortion and reflection, to listen to change in sounds, to feel the atmosphere. Activities in P.E. provide opportunities for pupils to observe and explore the body moving in space.

Pupils' ability to discriminate, to focus analyse, to justify choices and preferences and to make decisions will be extended by handling natural objects and making collections. Mirrors, magnifiers, viewfinders and tape recorders are useful devices to increase sensitivity to the natural world.

When considering functional design, what experiences are appropriate to develop an aesthetic and critical awareness?
Artefacts, systems and environments need to be considered from an aesthetic and functional viewpoint. Experimenting with function, sorting by agreed attribute, redesigning, making and evaluating will help pupils understand the differences between aesthetic and functional qualities. Collections of artefacts and walks in the built environment, for example, provide opportunities for pupils to discriminate between aesthetic responses and functional criteria.

In considering this issue it is felt necessary to re-emphasise the importance of working from first hand concrete experience and the importance of the learning process.

Resources should be chosen from a broad range of media which could include well illustrated fiction books, photographs, advertisements and works of art, craft and design from a diversity of cultures and periods.

Pupils' responses to direct experience may be supported and extended by discussing a range of works of art and craft. The works of art and craft might be introduced before the experience to give focus to the activity or after it to support pupils' making.

Pupils need to be aware that there are limitless solutions to visual problems.

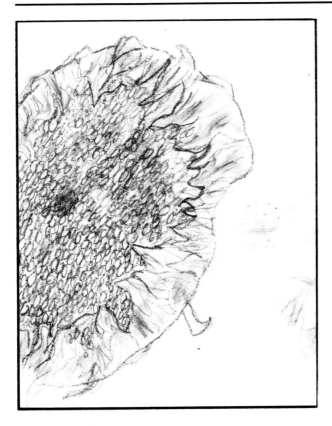

When considering art and craft what experiences are appropriate to develop aesthetic and critical awareness?

Pupil's responses to direct experience may be supported and extended by seeing and discussing a range of works of art, craft and design at first hand wherever possible. These works could include two and three dimensional works from different ages and cultures. The teacher could help the pupils understand the basic differences in the intention of the artist and the maker of functional design, and to consider the differences, if there are any, between their personal response to natural objects and to works of art.

The range of art explored should allow pupils to understand that the intention of an artist can be various. A work of art may be intended to be beautiful and to delight the senses; it may be to underline the horror of an event such as war. At this stage it may sometimes be appropriate to look at a work of art in its cultural context, but the importance of the

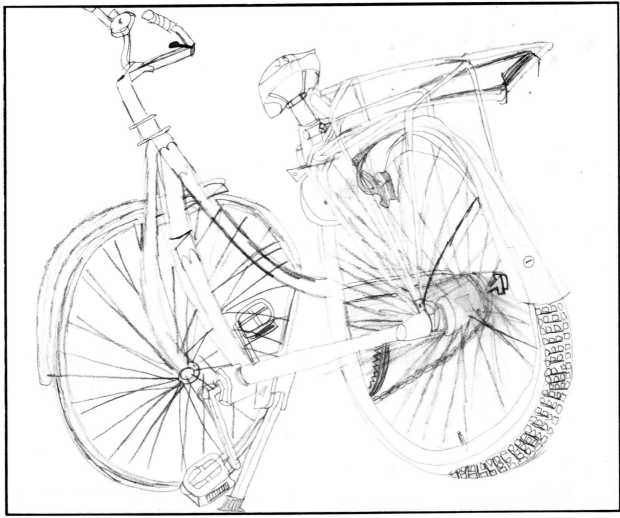

Key Stage 2 – Pupils' ability to discriminate and make decisions will be developed by observing and handling natural and made objects.

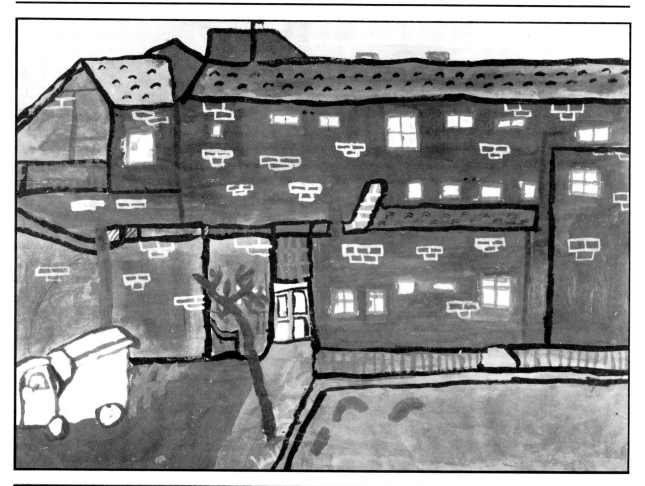

Key Stage 2 – Pupils responded to their environment and were then introduced to the works of Lowry.

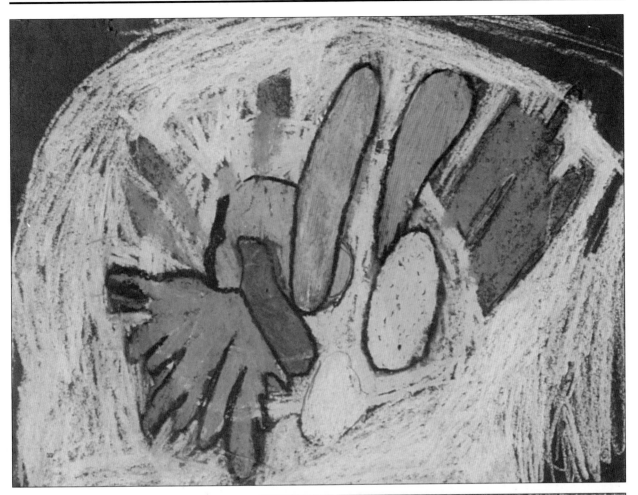

Key Stage 2 –
The work of Arcimboldo has
prompted an imaginative use
of observation drawing.

Key Stage 2 – Pupils have responded artistically and aesthetically to the direct experience of flowers.

Key Stage 2 – Using the work of other artists as a starting point, pupils have focussed on a small area of their environment. (plaster casts).

Key Stage 2 – A book illustration stimulated a figure drawing.

personal response to a work of art, which may develop with better aquaintance with a picture or with an artist, cannot be over-emphasised. The most important thing for the pupils to understand is that works of art are the expression of an idea which the artist is trying to communicate.

Pupils are best introduced to works of art in the context of their own explorations of the world. If they are studying the scientific aspect of water, for example, their experience may be expressed visually in their own work. The work of other artists from a variety of periods and styles may help them to understand that there are countless solutions to visual problems. The works of others might be introduced before their own observations, to help them focus their looking; when they have finished their work, to help them evaluate; or whilst they are working, to help them overcome a particular problem through seeing other possibilities. Copying works of art is not an appropriate way to learn about them at this stage, but pupils might begin to explore visually for themselves some of the ideas which have inspired other artists.

Works of art can also help children under-stand ideas in other areas of the curriculum such as history, geography and R.E.

Creating an ambience in the school

The rooms and corridors of the school at this Key Stage are traditionally a place in which the work of pupils is displayed to show that it is valued, and a place in which teachers arrange pictures, posters and artefacts to stimulate interest. This display is also often intended to enhance the appearance of the spaces, making the building a pleasanter place to be in. Displays could be set up with the purpose of stimulating sensory and aesthetic responses, extending the traditional 'colour' and 'feely' tables of the infant and first schools to promote deeper awareness and visual excitement. The displays could include works of art, craft and design in reproduction or original form, and include contributions which pupils themselves can make.

KEY STAGE 3. 11 – 14 years

Throughout the primary school the develop-ment of pupils' aesthetic awareness has been

Key Stage 3 – Design linking language and media studies.

based on their own responses to sensory experience. In the early years of secondary education this needs to be consolidated and developed towards a greater critical awareness in artistic terms. At this stage it is likely that there will be an overlap of responses that are of an aesthetic and artistic nature.

Pupils' perception of themselves and their world are influenced by the mass of visual communication that surrounds them. These influences, coupled with the "crisis of adolescence" creates new issues to be considered. Pupils will have the desire to work in a more sophisticated way but as yet may not be equipped with the skills, knowledge and understanding necessary to realise their ideas. Nor will the pupils have developed the ability to analyse their responses to the appeal of the mass media.

Teachers need to address not only the various levels of ability in terms of practical skills but also the varying degrees of ability to conceptualise. It is important that teachers use stimuli which relate to the pupils' cultural environment. This may be the means of entering their circle of activity. From the pupils' own responses teachers may move pupils into a broader arena when appropriate. When planning work teachers should make provision for the opportunity to begin to explore associations and meanings related to the subject matter.

At this stage we plan a strategy to develop aesthetic sensitivity and critical awareness through a variety of approaches. It is important to remind ourselves that these approaches are reflexive, integrated and overlap. When we respond to pupils we move from one approach to another. Vital to the development of pupils at this stage is a balance between aesthetic, functional and artistic learning experiences.

When considering the natural and made world, what experiences are appropriate to develop an aesthetic and critical awareness?
Pupils of a younger age are excited by and respond enthusiastically to natural and made stimuli. It is vital that pupils continue to be provided with opportunities to explore the natural and made world. In this phase pupils may, with growing adolescence, become increasingly self conscious. This may inhibit a spontaneity of personal response and consequent fear of articulating their response visually and verbally. Pupil's awareness may begin to show an appreciation of the abstract, conceptual level whilst still operating at a concrete level.

Teachers may help children use stimuli from the natural and made world which will elicit personal responses by constructing opportunities to explore the extraordinary in the ordinary. Such focused opportunities may consider

Key Stage 3 – "At this stage it is likely that there will be an overlap of responses that are of an aesthetic and artistic nature."

Key Stage 3 – It is important that teachers recognise stimuli which relate to the pupils' cultural environments.

exploring and playing with scale, size, similarities, differences, structures, textures, patterns. Pupils can be encouraged to discuss and discriminate between their discovery about the stimuli considering all the senses, their intentions and the development of a visual vocabulary.

When considering functional design, what experiences are appropriate to develop aesthetic and critical awareness?

As pupils become increasingly aware of the world beyond school and become more conscious of themselves in relation to that world, it is important for them to develop the ability to question and be curious about what they see around them. The mass of images associated with the marketing of products aimed at young people is designed to saturate their minds, making them potentially vulnerable consumers.

Critical awareness of functional design requires an understanding of:
– the properties of the material;
– the techniques which have been used to make it;
– the dynamics of visual language and form;
– a knowledge of the context in which the artefact will be used, and the context in which it was made;
– the constraints of the design brief;
– considerations of personal and aesthetic response;
– consideration of style.

The weighting of these criteria for appraisal will vary according to the historical and socio-economic context of the artefact. Pupils at this stage can and should begin to consider elements beyond their personal preferences.

Critical activities need to relate to the practical process which allows pupils the freedom and constraint to experiment, deviate, take risks, fail, make compromises and know that what has been created will be evaluated by appropriate and agreed criteria. These experiences will foster an understanding of design awareness.

Teachers need to consider how pupils' learning can be supported by an appraisal of what already exists, the use of designers in schools and links with industry through visits.

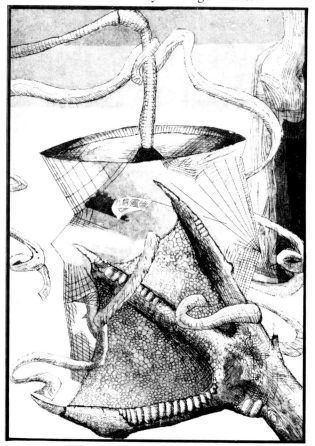

Key Stage 3 – At this stage pupils will reorganise observations to express ideas.
(aquatint)

When considering art and craft, what experiences are appropriate to develop an aesthetic and critical awareness?

Teachers have a responsibility to help pupils in this age group to become more discerning whilst encouraging them to explore their own visual identity. This may seem far removed from the study of professional artists and designers. However, by studying contemporary visual culture, pupils will begin to understand the power of images and art in society.

In addition to working from the "here and now", pupils may be introduced to examples of art and artefacts from other times and cultures. This should best take place when it reinforces and supports practical work in the classroom. When planning for particular learning outcomes we should consider whether such an input would be appropriate and if so, at what point during the work it would be most appropriate.

For example in a Year 8 project concerning the study of facial expression and identity, it would be appropriate to include references to caricature. However, if the subject is introduced by means of a slide show of Gillray's satirical work, the projects' purpose will be

Key Stage 3 – Children have designed and carved seats for their playground. A project with artist in residence, Robert Jakes.

copy, affect the way in which the subject is taught. The teacher may employ a practical, theoretical, analytical or hypothetical approach to create and develop situations that both extend and challenge pupils whilst meeting the examination requirements.

When considering the natural and made world, what experiences are appropriate to develop an aesthetic and critical awareness?

Teachers need to be aware of the pupils' familiarity with given or found stimuli. Teachers need to be able to negotiate and/or create experiences that empower pupils to recognise the potential of their own responses. Stimuli for aesthetic consideration should enable a re-discovery of the qualities of natural and made objects. To avoid a purely didactic approach pupils and teachers should share their experiences. This is not to say that the teacher will see the object as the pupil will. Teachers should avoid dominating and predetermining the pupils' responses with their own aesthetic and cultural perceptions. This will hopefully

Rich visual resources will stimulate ideas and responses.

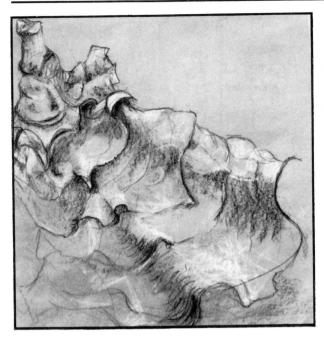

Key Stage 4 – "Stimuli for aesthetic considerations should enable a re-discovery of the qualities of natural and made objects."

encourage a recognition of the complex nature of the visual world and a respect for the diversity of responses likely to occur. Teachers will recognise the value in both immediate responses and more considered responses.

Natural or made stimuli may be approached through consideration of line, colour, sound, view points, texture, mass, space, associations, smell, taste and context. The pupils should be encouraged to develop the confidence to

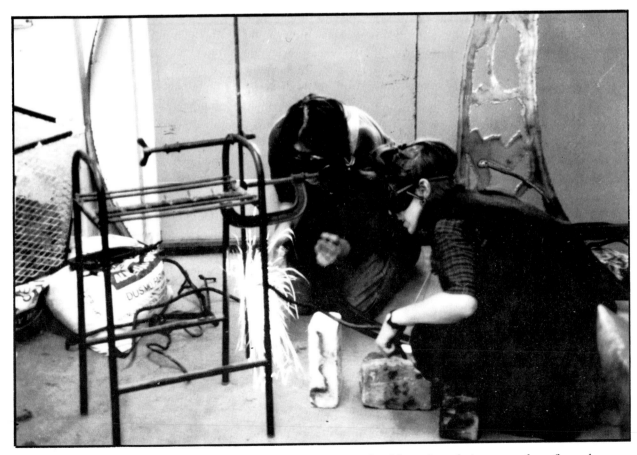

Key Stage 5 – Opportunities can occur at all stages to work with artists, designers and craftsworkers; a student works with artist Avril Wilson.

SECTION IV
Design
by Maurice Barrett

Dictionary definitions of the word "design" reflect the problem to be found in its use by different people in different circumstances. The main division is to be found between the practical and functional use of the word and its more open generalized use. Examples of the former are "a plan or sketch to work from" (Collins); "a drawing which shows how something is to be made" (Oxford Study Dictionary); and "the general form or arrangement of something" (Longmans). These differences arise from, or are the cause of, the divergency of approaches to design to be found within education. For the purpose of this paper

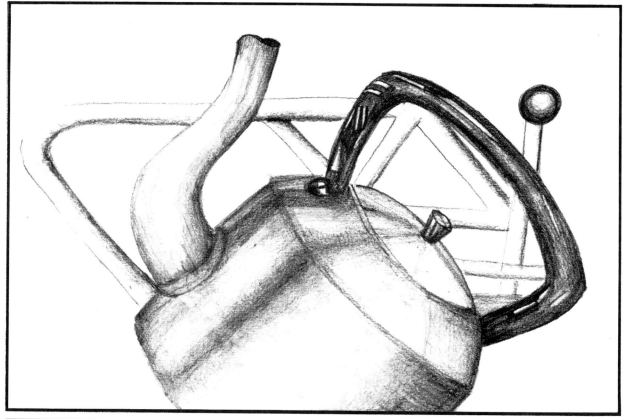

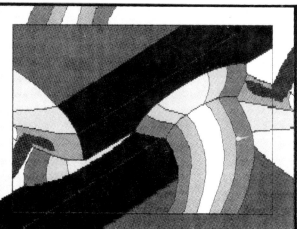

Key Stage 4 – Observational drawings provide the motif for the design on the T shirt.

we will use a simple abstract definition which will hopefully accommodate both the functional and openly creative forms:

"A design is the planning, drawing or forming of individual elements into a unified whole."

This definition will need to be elaborated to fit the context in which it is being used. In a work of art "design" is also the dynamic structuring of the elements used to embody the meaning of the work. In an industrial context "design" assumes that "function" is also an essential criterion. When used in interior design or fashion "style" may be an important

consideration. In all cases it is concerned with thinking about the positive process of making and the form in which that process is realised.

To make the definition too wide and general requires qualification when used in a specific context. To define it in a way limited to one aspect causes confusion and conflict. The Design Council's publication "Design Education at Secondary Level"[20] gives another broadly usable definition:

"To design is always to provide some form, structure, pattern or arrangement for a proposed thing, system or event. A design is always an integrated whole, a balanced prescription, a product of judgement and invention as well as skill."

This definition can accommodate the functional designer as well as the artist but the Design Council in "Design and Primary Education"[21] extends this and says:

"Design is the way in which we try to shape our environment, both in its whole and in its parts. Anyone setting out to design anything.....will be trying to mould the materials, space, time and other resources which are available to meet a need which she or he has identified."

This second quotation deals with design only in terms of "identifiable need". That is clearly in the realm of functional or behavioural objectives. While art, craft and design education will often be involved with this aspect of design it must not be seen exclusively in this form. In the area of craft, the materials may be manipulated for some aesthetic purpose which may not be functional. In art the pupils are concerned with the discipline of design in order to structure and embody meaning into the artefacts they produce. Design is the common denominator in all of these processes. The differences arise out of the intentions of the designer and the context within which he or she operates. Unfortunately, the 'contextualist' pressures within education today often place greater emphasis on learning through functional designing. The 'essentialist' approach holds that design has a distinct and valuable contribution in its own right and should not be subverted to other ends, no matter how desirable these may seem to be. It is worth mentioning that most designers are trained through art schools and art departments. The entry requirements are usually based upon the open ended art and design experiences common in primary and secondary school art curricula.

Ken Baynes has written extensively about design awareness and design in education. Coming from an art college background he has taken a much broader view of design than most writers. He writes about how children "encounter the natural and man-made worlds and how they first experience shaping their environment". He quotes Prof. Bruce Archer's[17] definition:

"Design is that area of human experience, skill and knowledge that reflects man's concern with the appreciation and adaptation of his surround-

ing in the light of his material and spiritual needs. In particular it relates with configuration, composition, meaning, value and purpose in man-made phenomena. The design area of education embraces all those activities and disciplines which are characterised by being anthropocentric, anthropological, aspirational and operational; that is, they are man-related, that have a value-seeking, feeling or judging aspect and that have a planning and making aspect."

Ken Baynes maintains that it is wrong to think of design as essentially practical. Like literature, science or art it is about knowing and speculating. But even this proviso is seen in the

Key Stage 1 – "Identify defects, needs and deficiencies."

Key Stage 1 – "Playing with possibilities."

context of "shaping the environment". Art is not only involved with design when we are making functional environments and purposeful objects. "Art, craft and design" as an educational discipline will always be involved with the process of planning, forming and making. But art is also concerned with a process of design in which the outcome has not been prescribed by a recognised need. Art is designing in the process of responding to perceptions. It is the process of giving visual form to our ideas, impulses, feelings and perceptions through the manipulation of media and materials. Any assumptions about design must include the value of designing in a non-utilitarian mode.

The emphasis within art and design education is towards creativity, defined by Jackson and Messick[18] as being involved with novelty and originality; appropriateness to context; transformation in the creation of new forms; condensation of many and diverse meanings into a product.

Lowenfeld[19], in his "construct for creativity" defines eight points which will serve the functional contextual approach as well as the essentialists who believe that designing in any context is intrinsically beneficial.

Sensitivity to Problems
Experience through senses;
We must promote sensitivity to problems and experience;
Identify defects, needs, deficiencies;
Recognise the unusual;
Refine our senses;
Recognise personal insight.

Fluency
Experimenting with alternatives;
Adapting;
Playing with possibilities;
Acceptance of variables and failures;
Fluency in the use of media and materials;
Design.

Flexibility
The avoidance of preconceptions as determining factors in finding a solution;
Adjustment to changing possibilities;
Avoidance of stereotypes;
Flexible use of materials.

Originality
The central and crucial element;
Uncommon responses to questions;

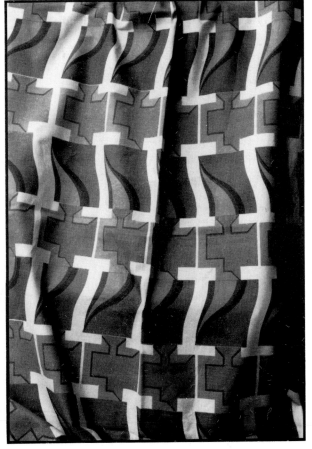

Key Stage 4 – "Adjustment to changing possibilities."

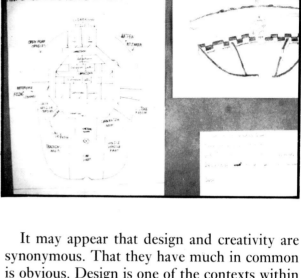

Key Stage 2 – "Uncommon solutions to problems."

Uncommon solutions to problems;
Independence of the ideas and solutions of
others.

Redefinition and Rearrangement
The ability to shift the function of objects;
The novel use of objects;
Avoiding preconceptions by redefinition.

Analysis or the ability to abstract
To penetrate the nature of experience;
The awareness of differences;
Abstracting from generalisation to form spe-
cific relationship.

Synthesis
The combining of elements to form a whole.

Coherence of organisation
Aesthetic experience is thinking, feeling and
perceiving resulting in a harmonious coherent
organisation.

It may appear that design and creativity are
synonymous. That they have much in common
is obvious. Design is one of the contexts within
which creativity can be fostered. In the school
curriculum there are many other disciplines
which provide opportunities for creativity.
Some would say that those which do not provide this opportunity are inhibiting the learning potential in that domain. Conversely design
could be seen as the underlying structure for
creative language work or the form of a dance
or a business strategy. It is best to view design
and creativity as reflexive parts of a learning
and making process.

At the central core of all subject disciplines
there is an aspect which is distinctly valuable in
a way that other subjects cannot provide. This
is how our subject based curriculum has
evolved. The value of the design approach to
be found in primary and secondary schools is
well established. The same can be claimed for
the craft orientated subjects. The fact that they

Key Stage 4 – "Sensitivity to experience."

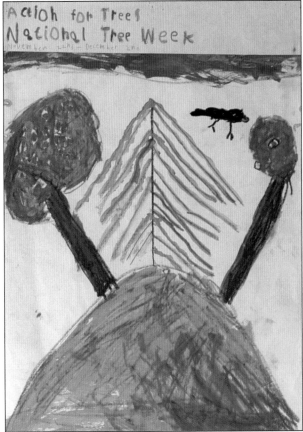

Key Stage 1 – A personal response to first hand experience provided the information to fulfil the requirements of a design brief.

Key Stage 2 –
At each key stage pupils need to
explore the design problems
inherent in a range of
materials.

Key Stage 4

Key Stage 4 – "Analysis or the ability to abstract to penetrate the nature of experience."

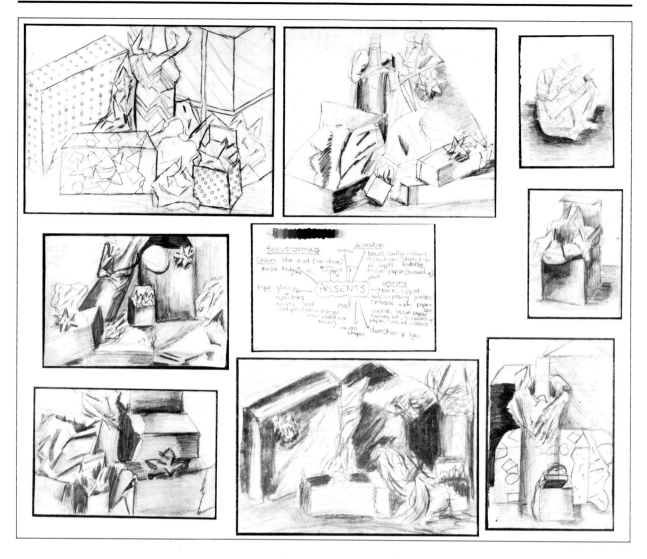

Key Stage 3 – "Planning and Making."

approach it from different stand points is an enriching benefit for the learners. This would be diminished if a common strategy were adopted in the name of consistency, as the child could be deprived of the enlightenment coming from diversity. It would be easier to reduce everything to the nearest common denominator but in the area of design this would be retrograde in its effect. Unfortunately the open ended essentialist approach of the art teacher is less easy to demonstrate to the layman than the objective functionalism of the technologist. We must continue to encourage pupils to learn through any process of design whether it is functional or artistic.

The Teachers' Discussions

Key Stage 1 – Disguising Red Riding Hood.

Having been involved with practical design activities, the teachers were then grouped into their particular phase of education and asked to discuss learning about design.

KEY STAGE 1.   5 – 7 years

In this phase pupils will be involved with design to make things which have a functional purpose, like a puppet with arms that move or a tower that will stand, or a cover to fit the doll's bed. They will also be designing in order to express their own personal ideas and feelings – a picture of me when I hurt my leg, or a clay model of our class gerbil, a collage of a frightening lion. Both sorts of design are worthwhile

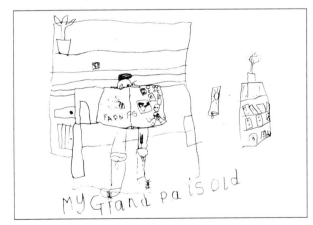

Key Stage 1 – Drawing Grandpa.
"Functional and expressive elements of design. The difference is the intention of the child at the outset."

Key Stage 1 – "It is through the manipulation of marks that pupils learn for themselves."

activities. The difference is the intention of the child at the outset. Sometimes one activity will include both functional and artistic aspects of design. For example, a child might make a puppet of a frightening lion with moving parts.

Children of this age are not consciously thinking about design when they produce work but once they have made their first mark on the paper they are designing. Subsequent marks, however random they may appear, have order and meaning for the pupil. It is through the manipulation of these marks that pupils learn, so they should never be told where to place any of them. This arrangement of marks within the frame of the paper (called a placement pattern), is so important to the design that the size or shape of the pupils' work should never be changed by an adult. The spaces that the pupils leave are as important an element of the work as the marks they make.

Young children are able to make definite decisions about the colours, shapes and textures they will use. When they have finished a piece of work they will resist encouragement to add more. Their decisions should be respected.

To encourage freshness of work, children should be given interesting and well organised materials and the appropriate tools for the job, e.g. clean paints, sorted junk, soft clay, suitable brushes, sharpened pencils, sharp scissors. If they are making a collage, a variety of fabrics and papers should be available and the appropriate adhesives provided. Pupils' design ability will develop through their own evaluation of the suitability of the materials and tools they have chosen. Are they happy with the results? Does the object they have made work? If pupils choose inappropriately, for example a biro pen to work on a large sheet of paper, they should not be demoralised by negative criticism, but encouraged to choose more effectively next time.

What is needed at this stage is experience of a range of materials and discussion of their effects. Which shaped bricks will build the highest tower? How can we stop the paint dripping when we paint at the easel? Where do I start to draw to get all the person in the picture?

KEY STAGE 2.   7 – 11 years

All artwork produced by pupils within this age range embodies design, subconsciously or con-

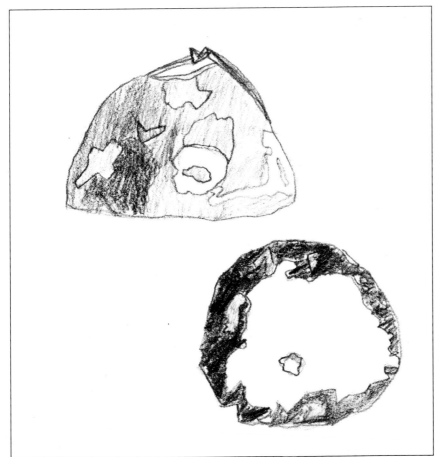

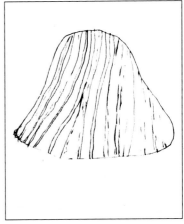

Key Stage 2 – "Children working with found objects to explore their characteristics."

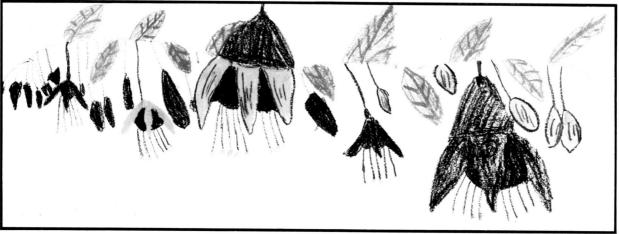

Key Stage 2 – "All art work embodies design subconciously or conciously. Childrens' new marks are dependant upon decisions they have made previously."

sciously. As they make marks upon a surface each subsequent decision taken is a considered response on their part to the initial marks made. The completed work is a result of this narrative process.

The differences between functional, aesthetic and artistic design need to be emphasised. For example, pupils working with found objects such as pebbles or sea shells are likely to explore their characteristics by feeling, drawing, talking and writing about them. They will initially respond aesthetically, expressing delight in qualities that they experience through the senses.

Further consideration of the shell as a home will bring in discussion of design features such as the structure which gives the shell its strength and could lead on to alternative designs embodying these characteristics. The experience of exploring the structure and shape of shells could inform the pupils' designs.

An exploration of the aesthetic qualities of the shell could provide the stimulus for an artistic response. The response may be extended into designing a motif for embroidery or printing.

All discussion at this stage should be handled sensitively, as described in previous sections. Such discussions could include reference to their initial stimulus, questioning their choice of materials or colour, intentions, problems encountered and alternative solutions.

Adequate time should be given to enable pupils to explore the potential of materials before arriving at a design solution.

A disciplined approach and level of commitment needs to be fostered. Pupils need to understand that materials impose their own limitations and discipline, and that perseverance may be needed to realise their ideas.

The attitude adopted by the teacher should always be one of encouragement and interested involvement rather than interference.

KEY STAGE 3.   11 – 14 years

Influences affecting pupils' perception of design in school

During the early years of secondary school, pupils' experiences of the curriculum tend to be fragmented into different subject areas. However, they find themselves using similar skills and processes across a variety of subjects. For example, certain mathematical concepts may be applied in science, music or geography. Pupils also find that they are asked to 'design' things in many subjects for a variety of reasons. It is not surprising to discover how "Design a poster for....." has replaced, "Draw a picture of....." in many other subjects ranging from health education to history. In pupils' minds, the two phrases are sometimes interchangeable in meaning, with the possible distinction being the addition of lettering in "Design a poster for.....".

In their technology lessons, pupils should become familiar with functional aspects of design and should be involved in the processes of generating designs, from identifying a need, to exploring alternative solutions and modifying or adapting ideas, through to the final outcome and evaluation of the successful fulfilment of the brief. If this is taking place in technology, to what extent is it necessary to plan for similar experiences of functional design in art?

Art teachers should clarify the meaning of 'design' and highlight the differences between designing for functional ends (external need) and expressive ends (internal need).

Influences affecting pupils' perception of design in society

In recent years the word 'designer' has been added to the title of any manufactured item to suggest either "superior quality" or "contemporary style" or simply "more expensive". One aspect of the crisis of adolescence is the need for children to be associated with the 'right' people by wearing the 'right' clothes and by equipping themselves with the 'right' gear, from school bags to bicycles. This makes them vulnerable consumers of 'designer' goods. 'Design' is confused with 'style' and the only

Key Stage 3 – "The finished design of any work of art is determined by the pupil's intentions. The outcome is influenced by the nature of the media." (Paper and paste)

Key Stages 4/5 – Designing integrates perceptions, visual form and decisions about media and materials.

style acceptable to the young consumer is that which is acceptable to the majority of the peer group. Should the art teacher try to ignore these influences? Is it possible to use them as a means of developing pupils' critical awareness of contemporary design?

Learning about design
Working from first hand observation of design in nature provides a valid starting point for learning about design for functional ends.

Nature's designs serve particular purposes connected with survival and have evolved to fulfil these purposes well. The diversity of design solutions in nature demonstrates the possibility and richness of alternatives. Our notion of 'elegant solutions' has developed through our observations of nature, where the most effective answer to a problem has a certain 'rightness' (or truth or beauty) about it. Adaptability to changing circumstances is essential to survival and demands modification of design.

Pupils should be offered opportunities to express ideas, impulses and feelings in which the specific nature of the media used will provide design problems.

The development of human technology has been based upon our understanding of design in the natural world and of natural forces. Pupils' awareness of the link may be fostered by asking them to find examples of objects made by humans which have parallels in nature. For example, packaging fragile objects/seed pods; transporting objects through the air without the aid of in-built propulsion/dandelion seeds/parachutes.

In addition to natural forces and materials, the human designer's raw materials include the elements of visual form. The artist/designer uses these to express a personal response to the world.

KEY STAGE 4/5.   14 – 18 years

In this phase they are developing a new maturity based on their relationship to their own peer group, cultural background and a move into the adult world of choice and discrimination. They are affected by change, cultural constraints, the reassessment of their own perceptions, and responses to the making and appraising of design through art.

It is important to understand what we mean by design in relation to the aesthetic, the functional and the artistic responses.

Aesthetic decisions would influence the design of a floral arrangement. William Morris's study of natural form was the stimulus for functional designs for fabrics and wallpapers. Vincent Van Gogh painted a vase of flowers with the artistic intention to communicate a personal vision through direct observation of the world around him. The placement of the flowers on the rectangular shape of the canvas, the choice of colours, the use of brush strokes are design decisions.

Design plays a fundamental part in any art activity. By design we do not mean a separate approach or body of knowledge, but the individual's perceptions and manipulation of visual form, the decisions made about media, material, techniques and their organisation in relation to impulses, feelings and ideas.

We do not see design as an end in itself but as a means of developing an awareness of the process and possibilities in investigating and making. Many pupils in this age group experience specific disciplines (textile design, graphic design, sculpture, 3D product design, painting, drawing and collage work), where the limitations of a brief may help the focus on a specific design problem. In order to create and enhance an atmosphere of lively inquiry within the classroom/studio/workshop, the teacher will need to direct attention by the display of objects and materials relevant to a particular pupil's needs.

Pupils may find that through researching many cultures, they become more critically aware and respond visually and artistically in an informed and more personal way.

Recognition of these qualities is clearly part of the design understanding we would wish to develop in pupils.

Key Stage 1 and 2 – Pupils investigate the company's problem, on site and through their own model.

Key Stages 3, 4 and 5 – Pupils research and develop ideas, explore the potential of materials and finally paint the hoardings. (Finch Group Project for K.S. 1–5)

A Final Comment

Throughout these guidelines there has been an emphasis upon the need to allow the pupils to explore their own reality and create their own solutions.

We need to keep in mind that there are two ways of inhibiting the pupils' creative imagination. The first will occur if we overburden the "explorer" with so many aids that they are not free to discover their own solutions. They will develop craft design skills, but their imaginative use could become restricted. The second inhibition can occur if the pupils have not been able to develop the skills required to give visual form to their own imagination. It is the teachers' task to respond to these two essential requirements. The balance between freedom and control is the greatest of our professional responsibilities. Total freedom can lead to anarchy; total control to dictatorship. Neither of these strategies, in isolation, can provide a useful guide to the process of learning.

Bibliography

Section I

1. Hampshire County Council (1986): "Guidelines for Art Education".

2 Department of Education & Science (1985): "National Criteria for Art & Design", HMSO.

3 Devon Education Authority, Working Party on Assessment of Achievement.

4 Treacher, Veronica: "Assessment and Evaluation in the Arts", Berkshire LEA's.

5 Pickard, Eileen (1979): "The Development of Creative Ability", National Foundation for Educational Research.

6 Department of Education & Science (1983): "Art in Secondary Education, 11–16", HMSO.

7 Journal of Art & Design Education, (Vol. 9, No 3., 1990).

Section II

8 Witkin, Robert (1974): "The Intelligence of Feeling" Heinemann Educational Books, London.

9 Parsons, Michael J. (1989): "How we understand art". Cambridge University Press.

10 Warnock, Mary (1983): In an essay on imagination in "The Arts, a way of knowing", Malcolm Ross (ed.) Pergamon Press.

11 Reid, Louis Arnaud (1980): "The intrinsic value of the arts in the education of children"; Journal of the National Society for Art Education.

12 Sausmarez, Maurice de (1964): "Basic Design: The dynamics of visual form." London, Cassell.

13 Ozenfant – source unknown.

14 Best, David (1981): Report on INSEA Conference, Rotterdam.

Section III

15 Alexander, Samuel, American philosopher; source unknown.

16 Reid, Louis Arnaud, (1981): "The Aesthetic Imperative" (ed.) Malcolm Ross, Pergamon Press.

Section IV

17 Archer, Bruce (1990): Quoted by Ken Baynes in "Defining a Design Dimension of the Curriculum" in "Issues in Design Education" (ed) D. Thistlewood. Longman/National Society for Education in Art & Design.

18 Jackson and Messick (1971): "Personality, Growth and Learning" Open University.

19 Lowenfeld, Victor and Lambert, Britain (1969): "Creative and Mental Growth" Fourth Edition, New York, Macmillan.

20 Design Council, "Design Education at Secondary Level", 1980.

21 Design Council, "Design and Primary Education", 1987.